DATE DUE			

THE METAMORPHOSIS OF LOPE DE VEGA'S KING PEDRO

(The Treatment of Pedro I de Castilla in the drama of Lope de Vega)

FRANCES EXUM
Winthrop College, S. C., U. S. A.

THE METAMORPHOSIS OF LOPE DE VEGA'S KING PEDRO

(THE TREATMENT OF PEDRO I DE CASTILLA IN THE DRAMA OF LOPE DE VEGA)

COLECCION	PLAZA MAYOR	SCHOLAR
PLAYOR, S. A.		MADRID

© 1974, Frances Exum
Depósito Legal: M. 17.852 - 1974
I S B N : 84 - 359 - 0160 - 2
Colección Plaza Mayor Scholar
PLAYOR, S. A.
Apartado 50.869, Madrid
PRINTED IN SPAIN
Impreso en España

PLAYOR, S. A. - Mar Menor, 16 - MADRID-33

To Dr. DOROTHY L. HOFFMAN,
With love and the deepest admiration.

TABLE OF CONTENTS

TABLE OF CONTENTS

INTRODUCTION

The Golden Age theater-going public in Spain was familiar with its national history and delighted in seeing well-
known historical characters and popular traditions reenact-
ed on the stage. Lope de Vega, the creator of the national
Spanish theater, and an artist highly responsive to popular
preferences, was the first poet to bring to the Spanish stage
the enigmatic character of Pedro I de Castilla (1350-1369),
sometimes known as «el justiciero» and sometimes as «el
cruel», a unique personality who had a special place in the
imagination of the Spanish people.

While there have been studies which deal in part with
Lope's treatment of Pedro I, [1] none has been dedicated solely to this purpose, nor does any one of them include a
detailed examination of all eight of the plays attributed to
Lope in which King Pedro I appears as a character. This is
the aim of the present study.

Of the seven plays dealing with Pedro I de Castilla which

---

[1] Lomba y Pedraja and Emily Schons offer a valuable interna-
tional bibliography of works dealing with Pedro. In these studies
there is also an interesting examination of the legendary material
used by Lope in the plays. Ebba Vockrodt includes Lope in her
study of several Golden Age playwrights who treated Pedro I in
their plays. Ballesteros includes an excellent bibliography of historical works on the reign of Pedro I.

are contained in Volume IX of the first Academy edition of
the works of Lope de Vega, [2] Menéndez y Pelayo considers
only *El rey don Pedro en Madrid, Los Ramírez de Arellano,
El médico de su honra,* and *La carbonera* to be historical
plays.   On the other hand, in *La niña de plata* and *Lo cierto por lo dudoso* (both *comedias de enredo*) Pedro plays
the role of a *galán* in a conventional love intrigue.

An eighth play which treats Pedro I, *Ya anda la de Mazagatos,* is included in Volume X of the new series of the
works of Lope de Vega published by the Royal Academy. [3]
Although similar in plot to the *comedias de enredo,* this
play may well be included among the historical dramas because of the preoccupation of the poet in portraying Pedro
as a *rey justiciero.*

Lope's method of adapting the historical facts of the
reign of Pedro I de Castilla to the drama includes frequent
anachronisms and incorporates legendary material that
would not be acceptable in a formal historical presentation.

Since the aim of the poet is not so much that of presenting a dramatized chronicle as it is to offer entertainment
and diversion to an audience well acquainted with its national history, these plays may not be judged according to the
same standards that one would use in evaluating a purely
historical document.

Lope's purpose is to entertain rather than to instruct his
audience.   He selects the historical material for each play
with an eye to its dramatic effectiveness.   Of necessity, his
portrayal of Pedro and other historical personalities in
the love intrigues of *La niña de plata* and *Lo cierto por lo*

---

[2]   Lope Félix de Vega y Carpio, *Obras,* Edited by Marcelino
Menéndez y Pelayo (15 vols.; Madrid: Real Academia Española,
1890-1913).
[3]   Lope Félix de Vega y Carpio, *Obras,* Edited by Emilio Cotarelo y Mori, *et al.* (13 vols.; Madrid: Real Academia Española,
1916-1930).

dudoso, while offering valuable insight into certain nuances of the poet's overall dramatic treament of Pedro, differs in degree of psychological penetration from his presentation in the historical dramas.

The poet telescopes events spanning almost the entire reign of Pedro I into his historical play *Los Ramírez de Arellano.* In *Audiencias del rey don Pedro, Ya anda la de Mazagatos, El médico de su honra,* and *La carbonera* Pedro's role as *rey justiciero* is an important element in the outcome of the dramatic plot, which has as its theme the Spanish Golden Age concept of honor. *El rey don Pedro en Madrid* is the only play in which the dramatic action is dominated by the personality of King Pedro, who is the source of all plot complication.

In the absence of autograph manuscripts of *El rey don Pedro en Madrid* and *El médico de su honra* there has been some controversy concerning their attribution to Lope. Although it is not the purpose of the present writer to attempt to prove the authorship of these plays or that of the *Audiencias del rey don Pedro* and *Ya anda la de Mazagatos,* which are also most commonly attributed to Lope, it is perhaps appropriate to state that she finds the persuasive arguments of Menéndez y Pelayo in favor of Lope's authorship to be the most convincing testimony until more positive proof is offered for their attribution to another playwright, hence their inclusion here.

El médico de su honra and *El rey don Pedro en Madrid o el Infanzón de Illescas* were published in the *Parte XXVII extravagante* of Barcelona in 1633. There are no complete extant copies of this *parte.* Menéndez y Pelayo used the most complete manuscript of *El médico* (Osuna tomo 133) as the basis for his text of the play in the Academy edition. A detailed study of the evidence for the attribution of *El rey don Pedro en Madrid* to Lope, Calderón, Tirso, and even Claramonte is found in the unpublished critical edition that

Sister Rosario María Asturias completed in 1964 at the University of Southern California.

The manuscript of the *Audiencias* that is in the Biblioteca Nacional de Madrid does not have the name of the author. Morley and Bruerton suggest as a range of dates for its composition between 1613 and 1630. They consider all three of the above-mentioned plays to be of doubtful authorship.

La niña de plata o el cortés galán was published in Madrid in 1617 in *Parte IX* of the works of Lope, prepared by the dramatist himself. It is included in the second list of the *Peregrino en su patria* (1618). Morley and Bruerton suggest as possible dates of composition between 1607 and 1612 (probably 1610-1612). The second *comedia de enredo*, *Lo cierto por lo dudoso*, was published in the *Parte XX* of 1625. It is not included in either list of the *Peregrino*. The dates of composition assigned to it by Morley and Bruerton are between 1612 and 1624 (probably 1620-1624).

A manuscript of *Ya anda la de Mazagatos* was edited by S. Griswold Morley in the *Bulletin Hispanique* (XXV, 212-225; XXVI, 97-191). The play is included in Volume X of the new Academy edition of Lope's works, into which the editor, Federico Ruiz Morcuende, incorporates the scholarship of Morley.

La carbonera, first published in *Parte XXII*, is included in Volume IX of the first Academy edition and in Volume X of the new Academy edition. The latter version substitutes the text of Act III from a manuscript in the Biblioteca Nacional. Morley and Bruerton suggest 1620 to 1626 (probably 1623-1626) as possible dates of composition.

Los Ramírez de Arellano was first published in *Parte XXIV* of the works of Lope de Vega in Zaragoza in 1641. It is included in the second list of the *Peregrino*. The dates 1597-1607 (probably 1604-1608) are offered by Morley and Bruerton for this play. In her edition of the play published in 1954, a descendant of the family, Diana Ramírez de Arellano, asserts that Menéndez y Pelayo did not use *Parte XXIV* when preparing this play for Volume IX of the Academy edition of Lope's works. She bases her assertion on the fact of several textual errors which do not appear in the *parte* but which he mentioned and commented upon in his critical remarks.

In this study we shall examine Lope's treatment of the medieval Castilian king Pedro I through a detailed examination of his eight King Pedro plays. We shall use as our text the two Academy editions of Lope's works. We shall also investigate the historical sources which would have been available to the dramatist and we shall discuss the manner in which Lope treated historical material in his plays. The reader may find helpful an alphabetical list of important individuals and a chronological outline of significant events of the reign of Pedro, I, which are included as an appendix to the text.

It is not the intention of the present writer to make general statements or to draw conclusions concerning the controversial historical figure, but rather to study in detail the development of the dramatic character Pedro I de Castilla as he appears in the eight plays included in this study.

an illustration for this play. In her edition of the play published in 1954, a descendant of the family, Diana Ramírez de Arellano, asserts that Menéndez y Pelayo did not use *Aore XXVII* when preparing this play for Volume IX of the Academy edition of Lope's works. She bases her assertion on the fact of several textual errors which do not appear in the *parte* but which he mentioned and commented upon in his critical remarks.

In this study we shall examine Lope's treatment of the medieval Castilian King Pedro I through a detailed examination of his eight King Pedro plays. We shall use as our text the two Academy editions of Lope's works. We shall also investigate the historical sources which would have been available to the dramatist and we shall discuss the manner in which Lope treated historical material in his plays. The reader may find helpful an alphabetical list of important individuals and a chronological outline of significant events of the reign of Pedro I, which are included as an appendix to the text.

It is not the intention of the present writer to make general statements or to draw conclusions concerning the controversial historical figure, but rather to study in detail the development of the dramatic character Pedro I de Castilla as he appears in the eight plays included in this study.

CHAPTER 1

THE HISTORICAL PEDRO IN CONTEMPORARY CHRONICLES AND BALLADS

The judgment of Pedro I de Castilla as either «el cruel» or «el justiciero» has been a source of continuing controversy among historians. The chronicle of Pedro López de Ayala, a contemporary of this enigmatic monarch, recounts dispassionately a long series of murders carried out by royal order. Ballad literature contains *romances* both favorable and unfavorable to him. Popular legends exist which credit him with a profound concern for justice and a love of the common man. Apologists have tried to justify even his most inexplicable deeds. Golden Age dramatists found him to be a subject offering varied interpretation and assured popularity.

In order for us to gain perspective for an appraisal of Lope's own literary creation we must first review some of these earlier judgments and representations of King Pedro. It is impossible to draw even the most tentative conclusions concerning the character and deeds of Pedro apart from a consideration of the customs and the temper of the age in which he lived.

In general, the fourteenth century was a turbulent and bloody era in European history. In particular, Castilla experienced a period marked by violence, unstable alliances and treachery at all levels of political activity. The pledged word alone was no assurance of compliance with the terms of an agreement, and hostages were often exchanged as security for alliances, even between sovereigns. Pedro I himself sent his three daughters as hostages to the Black Prince in 1366 as evidence of his good faith in their alliance.

In the words of Johan Huizinga in his book *The Waning of the Middle Ages* there was an underlying «spirit of revenge» evident not only in the political sphere, but also in the administration of public justice: «the Middle Ages knew but two extremes: the fulness of cruel punishment, and mercy.»[1] The dichotomy of severity and clemency so evident in Pedro's historical image is thus mirrored in the society in which he lived.

Closely related to his reputation as *justiciero* is the presentation of Pedro de Castilla as the defender of the common man against a tyrannical nobility. Medieval Castilian history contains a series of turbulent regencies with attendant power struggles on the part of the noblemen of the realm. The success of a king often depended as much upon his ability to subdue rebellious noblemen within his own territory as on his skill as a diplomat or military strategist in his dealings with other monarchs.

Feudal custom in medieval Castilla offers a paradox to the modern reader in that it is based upon sworn fealty between vassal and lord and yet it allows a nobleman to leave the service of his king and even join the ranks of an opposing ruler by going through the process of diffidation, or the renunciation of vassalage. A vassal could also leave the service of one lord and enter that of another simply by moving his residence from one place to another.

Behetrías were formed from territory not included in the royal patrimony but recently conquered by individual or

---

[1] Johan Huizinga, *The Waning of the Middle Ages* (London: Edward and Co., 1924), pp. 15-16.

group effort. In the *behetrías de mar a mar* the vassals could choose their lord freely, thus electing the one who could give them the best protection. In the *behetrías entre parientes* the vassal chose from among the members of one family group. This latter system was similar to the elective system of kingship in Germanic custom. It was more conducive to the maintenance of peace, since it reduced the possibility of feuding among rival noblemen.

At the *Cortes* of Valladolid in 1351 the young King Pedro and his chief minister Juan Alfonso de Alburquerque took steps to lessen the power of the often rebellious privileged classes. The reforms decreed by Pedro in these *Cortes* are one of the major reasons for his reputations as *justiciero*. Clearly-defined laws such as those contained in the *Ordenamiento de Alcalá* (1348) of Alfonso XI existed in theory, but were not enforced.

The people's only redress from their violation by the privileged classes was often a direct appeal to the king. There were abuses of power on the part of both noblemen and clergy: violation of *fueros*, seizure of Crown Lands, arbitrary arrest, judicial corruption, enforced labor in the lords' fields, unjust imprisonment and confiscation of personal property in the case of refusal, and even the threat of excommunication.

It is small wonder that this young prince, acting with the advice of his experienced minister Alburquerque, might come to be known as *justiciero* and champion of the common man for his actions against the privileged classes at the *Cortes* of Valladolid.

In order to understand the background of the young and inexperienced prince who so unexpectedly had thrust upon him the crown of Castilla, we must first acquaint ourselves with the members of his family. Pedro's mother, María de Portugal, daughter of Alfonso IV, was married to Alfonso XI de Castilla before the age of fifteen. She bore him two sons: Fernando, who died within a year of his birth, and Pedro, born August 30, 1334. María has been criticized by Ayala and others for her illicit relationship with the Portuguese nobleman Martín Alfonso Tello, whom Pedro ordered executed for his treachery at the rebellion of Toro in 1356.

On the other hand, in his book *Las mujeres del rey don Pedro I de Castilla* J. B. Sitges maintains that María, a faithful wife during the lifetime of her husband, was treated with respect by Alfonso XI, who sought her advice often in spite of his own liaison with Leonor de Guzmán. [2] Sitges refutes an often-repeated idea that María instilled in Pedro a hatred of Leonor de Guzmán and his bastard brothers. He also discounts the theory that a poison administered to María by her own father was the cause of her death at Evora on January 18, 1357. He states that Pedro was always respectful to her and to her memory in spite of her misdeeds.

The two deeds of María which are the most censurable are her ordering of the execution of Leonor de Guzmán, mistress of Alfonso XI de Castilla, which took place at Talavera in 1351, and her treachery in joining a rebellion against Pedro attempted in 1354 by the bastard brothers and led by Alburquerque, who had lost favor with Pedro in 1363 after the king took as his mistress María de Padilla.

Alfonso XI de Castilla, Pedro's father, is justly famous as a warrior-king in the struggle against the Moors. His most outstanding victory is that of Salado on October 30, 1340. Alfonso died of plague at age thirty-eight on March 23, 1350, while besieging Gibraltar. In his youth he also suffered a turbulent minority because of the death of his father Fernando IV only one year after his own birth. His grandmother, the capable María de Molina, served once again

---

[2]   J. B. Sitges, *Las mujeres del rey don Pedro I de Castilla* (Madrid: Sucesores de Rivadeneyra, 1910), pp. 53-54.

as regent of Castilla, as she had for her own son after the death of Sancho IV.

The one great disservice rendered by Alfonso XI to Castilla was his twenty-year affair with Leonor de Guzmán, who bore him ten children. One of the eldest surviving sons, Enrique, Conde de Trastamara, was later to become the murderer of his half-brother Pedro and subsequent King of Castilla.

Fadrique, Enrique's twin, was made a Maestre de Santiago at age nineteen by his father Alfonso XI. Fadrique supported Enrique in the Castilian civil war. He was murdered at Pedro's order in the Alcázar de Sevilla on May 29, 1358. The historical circumstances leading to the death of Fadrique are unclear and have given rise to theories concerning a possible liaison between Fadrique and the intended bride of Pedro, Blanca de Borbón, as we shall see later in our discussion of the ballads.

Another of the sons of Alfonso XI and Leonor de Guzmán was Tello, Señor de Viscaya, a title he gained with his marriage to Juana de Lara. Always seeking his own advantage, Tello treacherously served first Enrique then Pedro in their struggle for control of Castilla. Another son of Leonor and Alfonso was Sancho, a follower of his brother Enrique. The two youngest sons, Juan and Pedro, were put to death by Pedro de Castilla in 1359 after his defeat at Araviana.

Juana, the only daughter of Leonor and Alfonso, was married in 1357 to Fernando de Castro, a loyal supporter of Pedro de Castilla except for a period following Pedro's marriage and subsequent abandonment of his sister Juana de Castro in 1354.

Pedro was forgiving and even generous with his half-brothers on several occasions when they rebelled against him. In the first year of his reign, the young king fell seriously ill and was not expected to live. Since Pedro was the only legitimate heir of Alfonso XI, there was some question as to a successor, and rival factions sprang into being supporting the claims of Fernando de Aragón, nephew of Alfonso XI de Castilla, and those of Juan Núñez de Lara, great-grandson of Alfonso XI de Castilla. Although the bastard brothers were active in the ensuing intrigue, there is no evidence that Pedro bore them the resentment that he displayed in his later dealings with other nobles who had conspired to seize his throne while he was yet living.

In 1352 Enrique led an unsuccessful rebellion in Asturias. Against the advice of his principal minister Alburquerque, Pedro reconciled himself with Enrique and Tello when they attended his marriage to Blanca de Borbón in Valladolid on June 3, 1353. The following year Enrique and Fadrique joined a conspiracy to place Pedro de Portugal on the Castilian throne, thereby betraying the trust that Pedro had placed in them as newly-appointed *adelantados* of the Portuguese frontier.

The brothers also participated in the imprisonment of Pedro at Toro the same year after his meeting with the rebellious noblemen at the *Vistas* of Tejadillo. Pedro was again reconciled with Fadrique in 1356. Soon thereafter Enrique renounced Castilla and swore allegiance to her powerful enemy Pedro IV de Aragón in return for the latter's assistance in the civil war.

A highly interesting aspect of Pedro's life that was not developed by Lope de Vega in his plays concerning this monarch was his love for María de Padilla, who was his mistress from 1352 until her death in 1361. There are no historical documents to prove that Pedro and María were legally man and wife other than the king's own statement at the *Cortes* of Sevilla in 1362.

According to the marriage custom prior to the Tridentine pronouncement of 1563 which banned the practice of clandestine marriages, a man and woman who were free to marry were considered legally man and wife once they had taken a mutual vow and consummated the union. It would be, therefore, entirely possible for the liaison between Pedro and María to be considered a legal marriage were it not for the apparent absence of a public or private mutual statement of desire that it be so considered.

The only reason that Pedro gave for not revealing the «secret marriage» earlier was the fear of unsettling the people. A far more compelling reason in favor of announcing the supposed marriage at the time that he did might have been to provide Castilla with legitimate successors to the throne. As demonstrated by the registering of his will in 1362, Pedro was aware that he might die soon. His son Alfonso would need the support of legitimacy to strengthen his position as heir to the throne of Castilla.

If María was his legal wife, it is difficult to understand how Pedro could have allowed her to be considered his concubine for as long as she lived. Also, although his marriage to Blanca de Borbón was apparently not consummated, and was later declared null by the Bishops of Avila and Salamanca, María raised no objection to the performance of the ceremony, but patiently endured her role as mistress. Pedro was an unwilling groom, and he abandoned his bride two days after the marriage to return to María.

The reasons for this sudden departure of Pedro from the side of Blanca remain a mystery to historians. There is a contemporary ballad, one of the few favorable to Pedro, which tells of a liaison between Blanca and Pedro's half-brother Fadrique, and even suggests that a son was born of the supposed relationship. The historian Balles-teros notes in the third volume of his *Historia de España y su influencia en la historia universal* [3] that later genealo-

---

[3] Antonio Ballesteros y Beretta, *Historia de España y su influencia en la historia universal*, III (2nd ed.; Barcelona: Salvat Editores, S. A., 1948), 401-402.

gists claimed this son to be Alfonso Enríquez, admiral in
the time of Enrique III and great-grandfather of Fernando,
el Rey Católico, although there are no historical documents
to prove such an assertion.

Most historians, however, reject the idea of such a liaison. Other possible explanations which have been offered
for Pedro's abandonment of Blanca include non-payment
of dowry by the King of France (J. B. Sitges), Pedro's re-
jection of the policies of Alburquerque, who had been responsible for the marriage contract as an alliance with
France (Georges Cirot), and the overpowering passion of Pedro for his mistress María, who just prior to the wedding
had given birth to their first daughter (Juan de Mariana). A
popular legend contained in Mariana's *Historia de España* [4]
tells of a magic girdle given to Pedro by María which made
his new bride abhorrent to him.

J. B. Sitges writes that, according to papal correspond-
ence dating from April, 1354, María de Padilla requested
of Pope Innocent VI permission to enter a convent. [5] In
that same year Pedro, without requesting the necessary
papal dispensation, married Juana de Castro, his widowed
cousin and the half-sister of Inés de Castro. He left her
after one day to return to María de Padilla, declaring this
marriage null due to bonds of consanguinity. Possible
reasons for this action of Pedro range from the patching
up of a lovers' quarrel with María to suspicion of
involvement of Juana in the plot to place Pedro de Portugal
on the throne of Castilla. [6]

Although there were many other women in the life of
Pedro I, he never renounced his mistress María de Padilla,

---

[4] Juan de Mariana, *Historia de España,* BAE, XXX (Madrid:
Editorial Hernando, 1931), 487.
  [5] Sitges, p. 393.
  [6] Sitges, p. 409.

and on several occasions he returned to her side immediately after severing relations with another woman. Historians are unanimous in their appraisal of María as a woman of physical beauty and pleasant disposition who was innocent of any complicity in the intrigues of Pedro.

Pedro de Castilla was not the only fourteenth-century monarch to be known in history as both cruel and just. His contemporaries, Pedro I de Portugal and Pedro IV «el ceremonioso» de Aragón share this dubious distinction. Another contemporary, Carlos II de Navarra, has the epithet «el malo». As we shall see later in our discussion, Lope presents in his drama such monarchs as Pedro IV de Aragón and Carlos II de Navarra with the characteristics, both favorable and unfavorable, which historical records have attributed to them.

Three kings ruled Portugal during the nineteen-year reign of Pedro I de Castilla. Alfonso IV (1325-1357), was the maternal grandfather of Pedro de Castilla. Alfonso IV prevented his son and heir Pedro from accepting the crown of Castilla when it was offered to him by the rebels Alburquerque and Trastamara in 1354. He was also instrumental in the subsequent reconciliation of the brothers Pedro and Enrique. One of the most famous events of his reign was his ordering of the death of his son's mistress, Inés de Castro «for reasons of state» on January 7, 1355.

Upon the death of his father in 1357, Pedro I came to the throne filled with vengeance against the hired assassins of Inés. When he and Pedro de Castilla signed an agreement to exchange political prisioners who had taken refuge in one another's realm, the guilty parties were delivered to him. This vengeful monarch had the hearts of two of the men cut from their bodies while they were still alive. On January 18, 1360, Pedro de Portugal solemnly declared that he had been secretly married to Inés. He had her proclaimed queen and her children by him

were declared legitimate heirs to the throne. The action
of Pedro de Castilla with respect to María de Padilla at
Sevilla in 1362 may well have been inspired by this previous ceremony.

In 1366 when the victorious Enrique was proclaimed
King of Castilla at Calahorra and King Pedro was fleeing
Castilla, Pedro de Portugal refused him sanctuary. He
repudiated the betrothal of Pedro's daughter Beatriz to
the Portuguese heir Fernando. Fernando I (1367-1383)
was later to wage war on Enrique II Castilla with aspirations of his own to the Castilian throne.

Pedro IV «el ceremonioso» de Aragón (1336-1387) was
a powerful enemy of Pedro de Castilla. One great source
of conflict was the territory inherited by the former's step-
mother Leonor de Castilla and her two sons Fernando and
Juan, who had taken refuge with their relative Alfonso XI
in Castilla after the death of Alfonso IV de Aragón in 1336.
As observed by Sitges, the Aragonese historian Jerónimo de
Zurita shows no patriotic bias when he describes the per-
nicious character of Pedro, IV, whom he considers equally
as «cruel» as his Castilian contemporary. [7] In his *Examen
histórico-crítico del reinado de don Pedro de Castilla* Ferrer
del Río sees both as despots who are faced with the problem of subjugating a rebellious nobility. But he adds
that while Pedro de Aragón is seeking to bolster the power
of the throne, Pedro de Castilla has more selfish interests. [8]

Carlos II de Navarra (1343-1387), another contemporary
of Pedro de Castilla, earned his historical epithet «el malo»
because of his treachery in all diplomatic relationships. On
November 8, 1354, he had Carlos de la Cerda assassinated

---

[7] Sitges, p. 162.
[8] Antonio Ferrer del Río, *Exámen histórico-crítico del reinado
de don Pedro de Castilla* (3rd ed.; Madrid: Real Academia Española, 1863), p. 195.

because the King of France had made him count of a territory that he considered rightfully his. In 1361 he made an alliance with Pedro de Castilla which would have forced him to fight Pedro IV de Aragón. He repudiated this alliance to pledge support to the opposing forces of Aragón and Trastamara on April 25, 1934, at the Castle of Sos.

A few months later Carlos made a new alliance with Castilla and the Black Prince to allow the English to enter Castilla through Navarra. He then accepted a money payment and the promise of Logroño from Enrique to oppose their passage. His ingenious plan to extricate himself from this web of conflicting alliances was to have himself held «prisoner» at the Castle of Borja during the Battle of Nájera. He was then free to ally himself with the victor. As Sitges observes, [9] Carlos was in a most unenviable situation. The ruler of a kingdom inferior in size and political power to any of those surrounding it, he was forced to negotiate from a position of weakness, and his word was trusted by no one of the sovereigns with whom he conspired.

John II «the Good» of France arranged with Alburquerque and Pope Clement VI the marriage contract of 1352 between Blanca de Borbón and Pedro de Castilla. His son, Charles V «the Wise» (1356-1360) ruled in his place while he was a prisoner in London after the Battle of Poitiers. Charles supported Trastamara in order to have an ally against England as well as rid southern France of the dreaded *Compañías Blancas*, the marauding bands of adventurers composed of men returning from the Crusades who served as mercenaries. Charles allowed Trastamara to take refuge in France after the Battle of Nájera and he sent Bertrand Du Guesclin to aid Enrique against Pedro.

Pedro's espousal and later abandonment of Blanca de Borbón was a source of great concern to Clement VI,

---

[9]   Sitges, p. 164.

Innocent VI and Urban I, the French Popes who resided
at Avignon during Pedro's reign. Innocent VI excommuni-
cated Pedro and encouraged the rebels at Toledo, who were
loudly proclaiming Blanca's cause. Urban V agreed to ab-
solve the *Compañías Blancas* of their sins if they joined
Enrique, and he contributed a monetary donation to Trastamara.

Another contemporary of Pedro I de Castilla, Edward III
of England (1327-1377), had proposed to Alfonso XI an
alliance which included the betrothal of his daughter Jane
to the young Pedro. But the young princess died and the
alliance was never concluded. In 1366 the king and his
son the Prince of Wales agreed to aid Pedro, as the legitimate King of Castilla, against the usurper Trastamara.
After the victory of Nájera, Pedro was unable to fulfil his
monetary obligations to his English allies, and the alliance
ended.

Two sons of Edward III, the Duke of Lancaster and
the Duke of York, married Constanza and Isabel, the daughters of Pedro and María de Padilla. The Duke of Lancaster, husband of Constanza, aspired to the throne of Castilla in 1372. In 1388 Catalina, daughter of Lancaster and
Constanza, married Enrique III de Castilla, thus fusing the
two lines descending from Enrique de Trastamara and Pedro I de Castilla.

The most important source for the history of the reign
of Pedro I de Castilla is the contemporary chronicle of the
Chancellor of Castilla Pedro López de Ayala (1332-1407)
contained in the *Crónicas de los Reyes de Castilla*. The son
of Fernando Pérez de Ayala, *adelantado* of Murcia and friend
of Juan Alfonso de Alburquerque, the powerful minister of
Castilla in the early days of the reign of Pedro I, López de
Ayala served at Pedro's court as page in 1353. In 1354 at
the *Vistas* of Tejadillo, where his father Fernando was the

spokesman for the rebel noblemen, the younger Ayala served as page to Fernando de Aragón.

Ayala served Pedro in 1359 in the naval war with Aragón. He remained in Pedro's service until 1366, when the latter fled Castilla. Ayala then entered the service of Trastamara, fought at the Battle of Nájera, and was taken prisoner by the English. After being ransomed, he rejoined Enrique. During the reign of Juan I de Castilla, Ayala fought in the Battle of Aljubarrota in 1385, where he was again taken prisoner. He served as ambassador to France, rose to the post of Chancellor of Castilla under Enrique III, and died at an advanced age.

Ayala's chronicles cover the reigns of Pedro I, Enrique II, Juan I and part of that of Enrique III. Since he was a follower of Enrique de Trastamara, Ayala has often been accused of presenting only the more unfavorable aspects of Pedro's personality. He also has his defenders who laud his impartiality (Prosper Mérimée), and those who show the fallacies in the arguments of his detractors (Rafael de Floranes).

Menéndez y Pelayo states that the ballads concerning Pedro date from the fifteenth century and must have been inspired by Ayala's chronicle, although none of them is taken directly from his text. [10]

On the other hand, William J. Entwistle makes a strong case in an article [11] that all of these ballads may be *romances a noticia* contemporary with the events that they describe, and that they may have served as source material for Ayala as well as for the *Cuarta Crónica*. Entwistle

---

[10] Marcelino Menéndez y Pelayo, *Antología de poetas líricos castellanos*, XXIII (Santander: Consejo Superior de Investigaciones Científicas, 1944), 36.

[11] William J. Entwistle, «The *Romancero del Rey Don Pedro* in Ayala and the *'Cuarta Crónica General,'*»*Modern Language Review*, XXV (1930), 306-326.

bases this assertion upon a close study of the murders at
Pedro's order of Blanca de Borbón, Fadrique, and Juan de
Aragón, Señor de Viscaya, as they are found in Ayala, the
Cuarta Crónica and the ballads themselves.

There is little agreement among historians concerning
the place or the manner of the death of Blanca de Borbón.
Ayala hints at poison administered at Pedro's command. [12]
The *Cuarta Crónica* of Jiménez de Rada states that she was
garroted. [13] Mérimée suggests that it is likely that she may
have been one of the many who succumbed to the plague. [14]
Sitges supposes natural causes. [15]

Entwistle notes the similarity of detail between Ayala
and the chronicles, and he offers the explanation that the
popular ballads may have been Ayala's source, in which
case the chronicler may have relied upon rumor for an
event which he himself did not witness.

Entwistle notes that the account of the death of Fadrique in Ayala is totally different from the ballad versions, but he does not find this incompatible with his ar-
gument for the ballads' priority because of the possibility
that the historian may have in this instance used a different
source.

The ballads concerning the death of Fadrique depart
from the historical picture of María de Padilla and represent her as cruelly demanding his death, and then throwing
the head of the Maestre to a mastiff. Some of the versions
also refer to her supposed magical powers and attribute the
ferocity of Pedro to her evil potions and spells.

------

[12]   Pedro López de Ayala, *Crónica de Don Pedro Primero*, BAE,
LXVI (Madrid: Rivadeneyra, 1953), 512-513.
[13]   Rodrigo Jiménez de Rada, *La Crónica de España*, Colección
de documentos inéditos para la historia de España, CVI (reprint;
Madrid: Real Academia de la Historia, 1966), 77.
[14]   Prosper Mérimée, *Histoire de Don Pèdre Ier Roi de Castille*
(París: Charpentier, 1865), pp. 324-329.
[15]   Sitges, pp. 378-382.

Ayala himself witnessed many of the events described in his chronicle, but he had to draw from other sources for some of his material. The account of the murder of Juan de Aragón is similar in the ballad and in the chronicle, differing mainly in the ballad's use of the first person. Entwistle argues for the priority of the ballad, showing instances of assonance in Ayala's prose.

The view that the ballads concerning the Prior de San Juan are in reality a part of the ballad cycle of Pedro I is held by both Menéndez y Pelayo [16] and José R. Lomba y Pedraja. [17] Both scholars base their opinions upon an incident included in the *Cuarta Crónica* which tells of the Prior's murder at Toro. [18] In separate articles N. E. Gardiner [19] and Diego Catalán Menéndez Pidal [20] assert that these ballads refer not to Pedro but to Alfonso XI and were, therefore, the source rather than the result of the incident described in the *Cuarta Crónica*.

Extant ballad literature concerning Pedro is, in the main, unfavorable to this monarch. As Menéndez y Pelayo observes, [21] the King Pedro of Spanish ballad tradition appears as a tortured and tormented figure preoccupied with evil omens. This supernatural aura surrounding Pedro in the ballads is also an important element in Lope's dramatic technique in handling the character of King Pedro, as we shall see in our study of the drama.

Diego Catalán Menéndez Pidal tells of his discovery of a ballad favorable to Pedro which refers to the rebellion of

[16]   Menéndez y Pelayo, *Antología*, pp. 38-39.
[17]   José R. Lomba y Pedraja, «El Rey don Pedro en el teatro,» *Homenaje a Menéndez y Pelayo*, II (Madrid, 1899), 275.
[18]   Jiménez de Rada, pp. 90-91.
[19]   N. E. Gardiner, «The Ballads of the Prior de San Juan,» *Modern Language Review*, XXXIV (October, 1939), 550-556.
[20]   Diego Catalán Menénez Pidal, «Un romance histórico de Alfonso,» *Estudios dedicados a Menéndez Pidal*. VI (Madrid: Consejo Superior de Investigaciones Científicas, 1956), 259-285.
[21]   Menéndez y Pelayo, *Antología*, p. 36.

Juan de la Cerda.²²   Another ballad favorable to Pedro
is the one which suggests an illicit relationship between Fadrique and Blanca.   This *romance* is probably an example
of the vicious slander that must have been operating in
Pedro's camp as well as in that of the victorious Enrique.

There exist other contemporary chronicles besides Ayala and the *Cuarta Crónica* which treat the reign of Pedro I
de Castilla.   The chronicle of Pedro IV de Aragón, written
seven years before his death in 1387, presents Pedro in the
unfavorable light that one might expect of an avowed enemy.   Froissart's chronicle, which recounts the exploits of
the French adventurer Bertrand Du Guesclin, an ally of
Trastamara, shows Pedro as perverse and avaricious.   In
1366-1367 Froissart was at the court of the Black Prince at
Bordeaux, where he must have heard reports of these events
from those who had taken part in them.

The testimony of Pedro Fernández Niño, a nobleman in
the service of Pedro de Castilla, is included in the *Crónica
de Don Pedro Niño, Conde de Buelna* («el Victorial») composed by Gutierre Diez de Games in 1435.   He uses both
of the epithets «cruel» and «justiciero» in his description
of Pedro.²³

In the reign of Enrique III, Juan Rodríguez de Cuenca,
Dispensero Mayor of Leonor, the wife of Juan I, wrote the
Sumario de los reyes de España.   An anonymous author in
the following reign of Enrique IV altered the text of the
Sumario and inserted an allusion to a «lost» chronicle in
which Pedro was «fairly» represented, asserting that the
extant chronicle had been preserved in lieu of the «true»
one in order to justify the fratricide.   The theme of a lost

---

²² Diego Catalán Menéndez Pidal, «'Nunca viera jaboneros tan
bien vender su jabón', Romance histórico del rey don Pedro, del
año 1357,» *Boletín de la Real Academia Española*, XXXII (mayo
agosto, 1952), 233-245.
²³ Ferrer del Río, p. 210.

chronicle more favorable to Pedro is continued in the apology and genealogy of the Castillas by Pedro de Gratia Dei, Rey de Armas of the Reyes Católicos, who names Juan de Castro, Bishop of Jaen, as the chronicle's author.

Juan de Castro was Chaplain to Constanza, the daughter of Pedro and María de Padilla and wife of the Duke of Lancaster. The Duke would have had no small interest in Pedro's rehabilitation in order to further his own claims to the Castilian throne in 1372. The existence of a chronicle by Juan de Castro is also mentioned in some *coplas* by Francisco de Castilla, a descendant of one of the bastard lines of Pedro. Another illegitimate descendant, Diego de Castilla, glossed the work of Gratia Dei, and may have been the writer responsible for the original claim for the existence of the Juan de Castro chronicle.[24]

Zurita, the Aragonese historian, received permission from Felipe II in 1577 to reedit the chronicle of Ayala. His *enmiendas* and *adiciones* are contained in the Llaguno edition for the *Biblioteca de Autores Españoles*.[25] Zurita corresponded with Diego de Castilla concerning the supposed lost chronicle, and he rejected the idea of its existence.[26]

Ayala's chronicle remains the most direct and authoritative source for the events of the reign of Pedro I de Castilla. Later historians of his reign whose writings date from the second half of the fifteenth century onward rely upon this and other contemporary chronicles and ballads for their facts concerning the man and his deeds and use the archives to supply any new information not found therein.

Lope's choice of historical material for his King Pedro plays from the sources available to him is examined by Lomba y Pedraja in his article on King Pedro in the Spanish

---

[24] Sitges, pp. 30-31.
[25] Ayala, pp. v-ix.
[26] Sitges, p. 34.

drama and by Menéndez y Pelayo, editor of the first Academy edition of Lope's *Obras* (Vol. IX). A separate edition of Menéndez y Pelayo's valuable remarks concerning Lope's King Pedro plays may also be found in the fourth volume of his *Estudios sobre Lope de Vega,* published in 1949 by the Consejo Superior de Investigaciones Científicas.

It was necessary for the poet to keep his audience in mind at all times. He selected for each play only those aspects and events of Pedro's reign which he needed to achieve the desired effect. Intent upon the dramatic effectiveness of each scene, Lope is occasionally guilty of anachronisms and alteration of some historical facts.

The dramatic action of the plays *La niña de plata, Lo cierto por lo dudoso* and *El médico de su honra* may be considered as dating from the period 1353-1354, when Pedro and his half-brothers were newly-reconciled and apparently on at least temporarily friendly terms. Lomba y Pedraja [27] and Menéndez y Pelayo [28] concur in this opinion.

The *Cuarta Crónica* mentions four brothers who enjoyed the company of Pedro during the years 1353-1354: Enrique, Fadrique, Tello and Juan. [29] The identity of Juan appears problematical, since it would be more likely that the fourth companion of Pedro would be Sancho, who was two years nearer in age to the other half-brothers and who was known to be a close friend and companion to his brother Enrique.

Sitges gives the following birth dates for the nine sons of Alfonso XI and Leonor de Guzmán: Pedro de Aguilar, 1330; Sancho el Mudo; 1331; Enrique and Fadrique, 1333; Fernando, 1336; Tello, 1337; Sancho, 1339; Juan, 1341; and Pedro, 1345. [30] The only sons surviving into adulthood

---

[27]   Lomba y Pedraja, pp. 257-258.
[28]   Marcelino Menéndez y Pelayo, *Estudios sobre Lope de Vega* (6 vols; Madrid: Consejo Superior de Investigaciones Científicas, 1949), IV, 277.
[29]   Jiménez de Rada, p. 69.
[30]   Sitges, pp. 56-100.

were the twins Enrique and Fadrique, Tello, Sancho, Juan and Pedro.

Another complicating factor is the existence of one sister named Juana. Since her birth date is unknown, she may have been so near in age to Enrique, Fadrique and Tello that, since she was the only female born of the Alfonso-Leonor liaison, the chronicler could have erred with regard to her sex and included her in the brotherly escapades with the name of Juan.

In *La niña de plata,* although there is no conflict evident between Pedro and his half-brothers, the suggestion of a future split is made in the very first scene between Dorotea, the «niña», and her aunt. Teodora is of the opinion that Pedro's severity stems from a growing fear of the bastard brothers: «No fuera tan riguroso. / A no vivir sospechoso».

King Pedro presides over the closing scene of the play in which two marriages are decreed. Pedro states: «En llegando doña Blanca / Los dos seremos padrinos.» This reference to Blanca's arrival is anachronistic because the reconciliation of the brothers Pedro, Enrique and Fadrique, treated as an established fact in this play, did not take place until they came to Valladolid for the wedding in June, 1353.

The action of the play *Lo cierto por lo dudoso* is set against the background of the celebration of the *Día de San Juan.* Enrique is afraid to admit to Pedro that he is in love with a lady named Juana because he does not want to declare himself a rival of his brother the king. Enrique claims instead to be interested in a lady named Inés. He is banished by Pedro for this bit of deception later in the play.

King Pedro arranges with great secrecy his own betrothal ceremony to Juana, which the Archbishop will perform. He is frustrated when, through an error in the arrangements with the girl's father, Enrique takes his place in the ceremony. Pedro recognizes the betrothal and forgives his brother for violating his edict of banishment.

The tension between the brothers Pedro and Enrique is obvious throughout this play. Although on the surface it appears to be no more than the natural conflict arising from their rivalry for the affections of Juana, upon hearing the following complaint of Enrique concerning Pedro's advantage in the contest by virtue of his position as king, the audience would inevitably sense the deeper historical conflict which led to the tragedy of Montiel: «¿Quién no ha de hacer elección/ De quien más puede y más vale?» (I, ix).

As Menéndez y Pelayo observes, in this play «quedan lanzadas las semillas del odio entre los dos hermanos, que en *La niña de plata* todavía se mostraban bien avenidos.» [31]

Aside from the appearance in the play of the historical persons Pedro and Enrique, *El médico de su honra* contains only one allusion to historical events of Pedro's reign. In the second act Pedro mentions his proposed marriage to Blanca de Borbón and asks the advice of his brother Enrique concerning the match. There is, of course, no historical basis for such a conversation, since the marriage contract was arranged by Alburquerque and the historical accounts attest to Pedro's objection to the ceremony.

The estrangement of the brothers evident in *Lo cierto por lo dudoso* is also reflected in the prophetic scene in Act II of *El médico de su honra*, in which Pedro physically assaults his brother and cuts himself with Enrique's dagger.

In *Audiencias del rey don Pedro* Pedro is reconciled with his half-brother Tello, who remains in his service during the entire dramatic action. Enrique and Fadrique, who do not appear on stage, are the avowed enemies of Pedro throughout the play. The play's historical background

---

[31] Menéndez y Pelayo, *Estudios* p. 299.

includes events spanning the years 1354-1366. Lope disregards historical chronology in his introduction of these episodes into the drama.

When Pedro arrives in Sevilla early in the play, he has just escaped from Toro, an event which took place in 1354. Soon after his arrival, Pedro talks with a Maestre de Santiago who tells him that he has received letters from France telling of mounting support for Enrique, who has been proclaimed king and has already promised his supporters Castilian lands and titles.

Although he was in France as early as 1356, Enrique was not proclaimed king and did not dispense his «mercedes» until 1366, when he crossed into Castilla with Bertrand Du Guesclin and the *Compañías Blancas*.

In the second act Pedro refers to the death of the Moorish King Bermejo, an event which did not take place until 1362. In 1351 this Moorish leader usurped the throne of Muhammed V, King of Granada, who was an ally of Pedro. Bermejo allied himself with Pedro IV de Aragón, forcing Pedro de Castilla to make peace with Aragón so as not to be faced with two such powerful enemies. Once the peace terms with Aragón were settled, Pedro de Castilla went to the aid of his ally Muhammed V.

King Bermejo never made any formal agreement with Castilla concerning either his allegiance or his fateful interview with Pedro in 1362. By appearing before Pedro with rich gifts, Bermejo hoped to win his favor, but Pedro took advantage of the situation to rid himself of his troublesome enemy.

In the third act of the *Audiencias* Pedro says that the King of Aragón has broken their peace treaty and that Enrique and Beltrán Claquín (Du Guesclin) are invading Castilla from France. This event occurred in 1366. Another example of anachronism in the last act is the prophetic

dream that Pedro has concerning his death in 1369 at Montiel.

Lope's treatment of historical material in the *Audiencia;*
indicates his use of sources other than the chronicle of
Ayala. In the reference to Pedro's imprisonment at Toro,
the duration of four years in the play differs from the short
period allowed by Ayala. [32]

Menéndez y Pelayo suggests that Lope may have made
this error because of having read the manuscript of Gratia
Dei, in which the latter follows the details of the account
as found in the *Cuarta Crónica.* [33] The *Cuarta Crónica*
states that the duration of Pedro's incarceration was three
years. [34] Since Gratia Dei refers to the period of reconciliation of the brothers as four years, Lope may have confused the two periods of time.

In the first act Pedro arrives in Sevilla with Tello,
who has just helped him to escape from Toro. There is
an allusion to Tello's title of Señor de Viscaya, which he
held by virtue of his marriage to Juana de Lara: «Agrade-
cido/ De que le dio por rescate/ De Vizcaya el señorío.»
(I, i).

The historical Pedro had indeed made the arrangements
for this wedding, [35] but this had nothing to do with a reward
for Tello's help in the escape from Toro. There is no mention of Tello's assistance to Pedro in his escape either in
the chonicle of Ayala or in the genealogy of Gratia Dei. [36]
Lope may have taken this detail directly from the *Cuarta
Crónica* itself, which does mention the proffered county of

---

[32] Ayala, pp. 257-259.
[33] Menéndez y Pelayo, *Estudios,* p. 322.
[34] Jiménez de Rada, p. 75.
[35] Ayala, pp. 438-439.
[36] Pedro de Gratia Dei, «Historia del rey don Pedro y su descendencia, que es el linaje de los Castillas,» *Semanario erudito,*
XXVIII (Madrid: Valladares, 1788), 224-268.

Vizcaya,[37] or from Mariana, who also states that Tello was guarding Pedro on the day of his escape and that he accompanied him. [38]

Further evidence that Lope may have been influenced by Gratia Dei is found in Lope's reference to a supposed regency of Enrique during Pedro's minority. This erroneous detail is absent from the *Cuarta Crónica*, but is contained in the genealogy of Gratia Dei, who attributes the supposed regency to all of the bastard brothers and not solely to Enrique.

Menéndez y Pelayo notes the similarity between Lope's account of the killing of King Bermejo and the version of Gratia Dei. [39] The same justification for the deed is found in both: that Pedro was avenging a broken pledge of support on the part of the Moorish usurper.

In her unpublished dissertation «New Material on the Dramatic Treatment of Peter the Cruel of Castile and the Diffusion of the Legend in France, Germany and England» (Chicago, 1933), Emily Schons discusses further evidence of the influence of Gratia Dei in the *Audiencias* of Lope.

Since Gratia Dei was writing a history of the descendants of Pedro, he does not mention the young Alfonso, son of Pedro and María de Padilla, who was born in 1359 and died early, leaving no heirs. On the other hand, he devotes special attention to a son named Juan, who was born sometime in 1355 of the brief union of Pedro and Juana de Castro, and who became an important ancestor to many who were claiming descent from Pedro de Castilla.

When Pedro states in the play that he had invited the Moorish king to the baptismal ceremony for his son

---

[37]   Jiménez de Rada, pp. 75-76.
[38]   Mariana, p. 444.
[39]   Menéndez y Pelayo, *Estudios*, p. 322,

Juan, there is clearly an error in names, since it was Alfonso whose birth date coincides with Pedro's dealings with the Moorish king.

There are no historical references to the events of the reign of Pedro de Castilla in the play *Ya anda la de Mazagatos*. The only historical character other than Pedro who appears in the play is Alvaro Pérez de Guzmán, but his role bears no resemblance to actual history. In the play Alvaro is presented as the father of a young noblewoman who is involved in a typical *capa y espada* honor conflict in which Pedro's role as *rey justiciero* is essential to the resolution of the plot, although he is not a major character in the dramatic action.

The only historical characters who appear in Lope's *La carbonera* are Pedro and his half-sister Juana de Guzmán, who appears with the name of Leonor. It is interesting that Lope chooses for the sister in this play the same name as the mother of the half-brothers.

J. B. Sitges describes in detail the two marriages and the misdeeds of Juana. She became the wife of Fernando de Castro in 1354, but was abandoned by him and underwent an annullment of the marriage shortly thereafter. Her subsequent behavior was «bastante censurable, hasta el punto de que su hermano Don Enrique mató por su propia mano a uno de sus amantes, aquel Pedro Carrillo que tantos servicios prestó a Trastamara.»[10] In 1366 she married Felipe de Castro of Aragón, whom she survived by several years.

The action of *El rey don Pedro en Madrid o el Infante de Illescas* appears to correspond to the relatively stable period of 1355-1357 when, although he was faced with the rebellion of the half-brothers, Pedro was still firmly in control of his throne and had not yet begun to show the most

---

[10]   Sitges, p. 56.

extreme vengeance which led to the murders of Fadrique and Juan de Aragón in 1358 and of Leonor de Castilla and the youngest bastard brothers Juan and Pedro in 1359.

In Act I Pedro mentions the possibility of a conspiracy between Blanca de Borbón and the half-brothers, attributing a ghostly visit he has experienced to a trick on their part. It was in 1355 that Pedro retook Toledo after the rebellion of the nobles in the name of Blanca. [41]

In Act III Pedro again mentions the conspiracies of Fadrique, Tello and Enrique. He is reconciled with Enrique at the end of the play, an event which would have been impossible after the Conde's flight to France in 1356, but which could reflect instead the reconciliation between Pedro and Fadrique which took place in the same year. [42]

In Act I the Infanzón mentions María de Padilla, insinuating that she and King Pedro are living in sin. Pedro angrily states that she is the legitimate queen, an assertion which recalls the action in the Cortes in Sevilla in 1362 when Pedro declared the deceased María his legitimate wife. [43]

Act I of Los Ramírez de Arellano opens as Juan Ramírez is saying goodbye to his sweetheart Elvira before leaving for battle in the service of her uncle Carlos II de Navarra. Juan Ramírez succeeds in killing the Moorish King Alid and wins the battle. King Pedro IV de Aragón then requests his aid in the conquest of Valencia. Enrique de Trastamara also asks for his support in his struggle against his brother King Pedro de Castilla.

Juan Ramírez receives a letter from Pedro which requests that he enter his service and either capture or kill Enrique as he passes through Navarra on his way to France. This act ends when the third king named Pedro, Pe-

[41]   Ayala, pp. 446-448.
[42]   Ayala, pp. 469-470.
[43]   Ayala, pp. 519-520.

dro I de Portugal, also seeks his aid. Juan Ramírez requests and receives permission from his king, Carlos de
Navarra, to serve Pedro IV de Aragón.

In Act II Juan Ramírez wins the support of his rivals
at court by his generosity and nobility. He leads the attack on the city of Valencia. In Act III Juan Ramírez
asks permission of Pedro IV de Aragón to enter the service
of Enrique de Trastamara. The Pope requests a meeting
between Enrique and the Kings of Aragón and Navarra.
Juan Ramírez is to oversee the castle in which the meeting
will be held. Don Juan refuses to help the monarchs in
their plot to kill Enrique, whom he allows to escape.

Pedro I de Castilla and the Prince of Wales discuss the
prophetic dream that a priest had concerning the death
of King Pedro at the hands of Enrique. Confident of victory, Enrique promises rewards to his supporters even before the battle. At Montiel, Pedro takes refuge in the Castle. Mendo Rodríguez de Sanabria tries to arrange with the
Frenchman Beltrán Claquín (Bertrand Du Guesclin) to let
Pedro escape. Claquín pretends to agree, but instead sets
a trap for Pedro. When Pedro's death is announced all
supporters of Enrique are granted their promised rewards.

The historical persons who appear as characters in this
drama include: Juan Ramírez de Arellano, Carlos II de Navarra, Pedro IV de Aragón, Enrique de Trastamara, Pedro I
de Castilla, the Prince of Wales, Bertrand Du Guesclin, the
Conde de Rueda (Francisco de Perellós), Mendo Rodríguez
de Sanabria and Gonzalo de Mexía, a Maestre de Santiago.
A brother of Juan Ramírez mentioned by Ayala does not
appear in Lope's drama.

Ayala records that at the Castle of Sos Juan Ramírez
de Arellano refused to aid the Kings of Navarra and Aragón
in the murder of Enrique. [44] Viewed in terms of the practi-

---

[44]   Ayala, p. 530.

cal realities of the historical situation, it would seem incongruous for the royal allies of Trastamara to be plotting against his life.

Menéndez y Pelayo, relying for his evidence upon the text of a pact quoted by the Aragonese historian Zurita, is of the opinion that Ayala confused this meeting with another held at the Castle of Uncastillo on August 25, 1363, at which the intended victim was King Pedro and the principal conspirators were Trastamara, Pedro IV and Carlos II. [45]

Ballesteros mentions three different meetings involving Carlos II, Pedro IV and Enrique de Trastamara which took place during the period 1363-1364. [46] Carlos II and Pedro IV met at the Castle of Sos in 1363 to discuss the offer of territory by Pedro de Castilla in return for the murder of Enrique, but the plan was not put into action.

The meeting of Uncastillo on August 25, 1363 involved Carlos II, Pedro IV and Enrique, who were in alliance against King Pedro. A second agreement at Sos between Pedro IV and Trastamara was signed in 1364. At this time Carlos II had decided to ally himself, temporarily at least, with the Prince of Wales and Pedro de Castilla.

Lope combines historical events and resolves anachronisms by not making definite references to dates or places in *Los Ramírez de Arellano.*

Ayala's chronicle first mentions the Castilian-English alliance in 1363. Enrique arrived in Navarra in 1356. Ayala writes of the appearance of the priest to Pedro in the year 1360, when the Prince of Wales might well have been with Pedro, but the scene at Montiel did not take place until 1369, two years after Edward had withdrawn his support. It would have been impossible for him to have been there, since he was seriously ill and died soon after he left Spain.

---

[45]   Menéndez y Pelayo, *Estudios,* p. 406.
[46]   Ballesteros, p. 69.

Enrique and his forces did not actually plan their attack on Pedro at Montiel, since they had been unaware of his position. The encounter came as a surprise to both parties. Enrique dispensed his famous «mercedes» in 1366 when he was proclaimed king in Calahorra and held *Cortes* in Burgos. In this play Lope shows him thusly engaged in 1369 in Toledo, which Enrique was besieging that year.

An interesting historical error is found in the closing scene of Act I when the third Pedro who solicits the aid of Juan Ramírez is said to be warring with his son over the latter's insistence upon marrying Inés de Castro. The father referred to here is, of course, not Pedro but Alfonso IV de Portugal. It is the son who is named Pedro. Inés died «for reasons of state» on January 7, 1355.

Pedro I de Portugal came to the throne in the year 1357. It was not until June 12, 1360 that Pedro had the body of Inés disinterred and crowned legitimate queen. If the action of Act I is taking place in 1356, when Enrique was in Navarra, then Inés was already dead but not yet the formally recognized wife of Pedro.

Menéndez y Pelayo notes that the list of grievances against Pedro that Enrique enumerates in Act I comes directly from Chapters I, II, IV and VI of the first year and Chapter III of the second year of Ayala's chronicle. He observes that Lope attributes even more crimes to Pedro than does Ayala. [47]

Among these is the death of Leonor de Guzmán, which Ayala attributes solely to Pedro's mother, the scorned wife of Alfonso XI. [48] There is no literary or historical precedent for Lope's attribution of this crime to Pedro either in this play or in *La niña de plata* and *La carbonera,* in which he repeats the error.

---

[47] Menéndez y Pelayo, *Estudios,* p. 376.
[48] Ayala, pp. 412-413.

Enrique tells Juan Ramírez in Act I that he had seen his mother the day before her death and that she wept and told him that she knew that she would never see him again. In Ayala the last son to see Leonor alive is not Enrique but Fadrique. Since Ayala's account makes numerous references to the Maestre, Lope could not have been making an error in changing from Fadrique to Enrique. He simply borrowed an effective scene from the chronicle and used it to gain sympathy for Enrique.

Historically, the last time that Enrique saw his mother was in Sevilla when she arranged to have him come to her apartments and there consummate his marriage to the twelve-year-old Juana de Manuel, thus preventing her possible espousal to either Pedro or to the Infante Fernando de Aragón. According to Ayala it was Pedro himself who gave permission for Fadrique to visit his mother at Talavera. [49] Had he been planning her death, it would seem unlikely that Pedro would have permitted such an interview.

Los Ramírez de Arellano is the only play of Lope de Vega which treats the actual death of Pedro at Montiel. As is usual in the Golden Age *comedia*, the violent act takes place off-stage and the event is described by an eye-witness. Mariana adds an element absent from Ayala's account: the assistance given to Enrique in his death-struggle with Pedro by «Beltran, que les dio vuelta y le puso (a Enrique) encima.» [50]

According to the research of Lomba y Pedraja, the assistance of Bertrand Du Guesclin and the famous words: «Ni quito ni pongo Rey, pero ayudo a mi señor» which came to be associated with the supposed act in later Golden Age drama, were first attributed to a follower of Enrique

---

[49] Ayala, p. 412.
[50] Mariana, p. 519.

named Fernán Pérez de Andrada, and later came to be associated with the better-known Frenchman.[51]

A curious error in his study is Lomba y Pedraja's assertion that Lope does not mention Du Guesclin's aid to Enrique. Since Ayala is silent on the subject of any aid given to
Enrique in the fratricide, the matter is still open to question.

Lope's presentation of the kings Carlos II de Navarra
and Pedro IV de Aragón in *Los Ramírez de Arellano* is faithful to their historical image. The arrogance and credulity
of Carlos II and his ingratitude toward Juan Ramírez are
shown in Act I when this king listens to evil advisers at
court. Pedro IV is reluctant to allow Juan Ramírez to leave
his service in order to fulfil his promise of assistance to
Enrique de Trastamara.

Juan Ramírez himself complains of the king's ingratitude
after he is abruptly dismissed from the royal presence.
Both of these kings treacherously plot in Act III the death
of Enrique de Trastamara and they try to convince Juan
Ramírez to violate his pledge to Enrique in order to aid
them.

It is an undisputed historical fact that Pedro IV de
Aragón was an enemy of Pedro I de Castilla and an ally of
Enrique de Trastamara. Why did Lope decide to change his
allegiance in this play? The simplest and most probable
explanation is that Lope aligned this unsympathetically
portrayed monarch with Pedro I de Castilla in order to
heighten the contrast between the nobility of the followers
of Trastamara and the duplicity of the royal defenders of
Pedro's legitimate claim.

Having had no success at winning the support of Juan
Ramírez, the kings try to convince him to allow another to
murder Enrique in the Castle, the security of which is his

---

[51]   Lomba y Pedraja, pp. 336-337.

responsibility.   Carlos even tries to bribe him.   Juan Ramírez bars the door and refuses to allow the kings themselves to talk with Enrique, saying that he is protecting
their honor by not allowing them to perform so heinous a
deed.

In this scene Lope contrasts the selfishness and treachery of two kings with the loyalty and the sense of personal honor of Juan Ramírez.   Enrique's cause is enhanced
by means of this glorification of his supporter, while the
reputation of Pedro de Castilla, denigrated long before he
even appears onstage, is prejudiced further by such an ex-
hibition of the negative qualities of the two legitimate monarchs who are defending him.

CHAPTER II

THE DIVINE RIGHT OF KINGS VS. THE RIGHT OF RESISTANCE

The seventeenth-century Spanish concept of kingship which is mirrored in the national drama of the Golden Age is in sharp contrast to the historical reality of the power and prestige of medieval rulers. In his historical plays, Lope de Vega invests even medieval rulers with the position and privileges enjoyed by Hapsburg monarchs. The result is the presentation of medieval events and personalities taken out of their own political framework and interpreted in the light of Golden Age ideals and seventeenth-century political theory.

Nowhere is this tendency more evident than in Lope's treatment of the controversial King Pedro I de Castilla. In order to appreciate the reasons for such an anachronistic interpretation, one must take into consideration: 1. the evolution of monarchical absolutism in Spain; 2. the parallel development of the doctrine of non-resistance to the monarch inherent in the theory of the Divine Right of Kings; and 3. both medieval and sixteenth-century ideas of the right of resistance against a tyrannical ruler.

Medieval political theory represents a combination of political principles inherited from the ancient world and

many customs and traditions of the barbarian peoples. [1]
There is a close relationship between medieval politics
and theology. In keeping with the ancient view of the
origin of human society and government as a divine remedy
for the Fall of man, St. Augustine conceived of the ruler
as an instrument of God. A wicked ruler might be given
by Him as punishment to a wicked people.

   In St. Paul's letter to Romans he says that civil
goverment is of divine inspiration and to resist it is to resist
God. The Christian has therefore a religious obligation
to obey civil authority. Pope Gregory VII went so far as
to state that a good people will not resist even an evil ruler. This view, quoted later by proponents of the theory of
the Divine Right of Kings, was very different from the
medieval principle of the supremacy of the law. The theory
of monarchical absolutism which derives from Roman law
does not contain the Germanic idea of the right of resistance of the people to an abuse of power on the part of the
ruler.

   This medieval right of resistance was based upon the
feudal concept of a mutual fealty binding upon both subject
and sovereign. The agreement became void if the king
failed to fulfil his duty to the people, and he was no longer
recognized as their ruler. St. Isidore makes a clear distinction between a king and a tyrant. A king ceases to
be king if he does not obey his own laws, since these laws
represent an expression of the customs of the community,

   [1] In her present discussion, this writer is indebted to the six-
volume study of Robert S. Carlyle and A. J. Carlyle, *A History of
Medieval Political Theory in the West* (Edinburgh and London:
Blackwood and Sons, 1930-1938), and to the scholarship of Fritz
Kern in *Kingship and law in the Middle Ages* (Oxford: Basil Black-
well, 1939), and of Ernst H. Kantorowicz in *The King's Two Bodies:
A Study in Medieval Theology* (Princeton University Press, 1957).
The text of this chapter will appear as an article in the September,
1974 issue of *Hispania*.

and are formulated with the counsel of wise men and the consent of the people.

Medieval monarchy was dependent upon both divine authority and popular mandate. On the other hand, the later view of the Divine Right of Kings attributed to the individual prince the authority which had previously belonged to the monarchy as a whole. The hereditary right of the individual ruler was thus conceived to derive directly from God without any participation of the popular will.

The principle of monarchical absolutism in Spain developed gradually from the time of Alfonso X, who advocated the establishment of a clearly-defined hereditary succession in Castilla. Neither Germanic nor ecclesiastical law contained either the idea of hereditary rule or the principle of legitimacy. According to Visigothic custom, the people chose from among the male members of the king's family the son or brother whom they considered to be the best leader.

The emergence of the principle of monarchical absolutism is obvious in the *Siete Partidas*, a fact which is in part the result of a reawakened interest in the study of Roman law. In Roman law the prince is sole legislator and an absolute monarch superior to the law itself, an idea a totally alien to medieval theory. The imposition of this concept upon Spanish political theory, which had been developing under the dominant influence of Visigothic law and custom, changed the course of its normal development. [2]

Monarchical absolutism in Spain gained impetus under the consolidated rule of the Catholic Kings. The Hapsburg dynasty saw both the culmination of Spain's power and prestige and the triumph of the concept of kingship by Divine Right. According to this theory, the institution of monarchy is of divine origin; hereditary right may not

---

[2] Marie Madden, *Political Theory and Law in Medieval Spain* (New York: Fordham University Press, 1930), p. 187.

be questioned; resistance to the king is sinful; and the king is accountable only to God. [3] It is this principle that is reflected in the profoundly monarchical sentiment of the drama of the Spanish Golden Age.

The decline of Spain from her position as a world power during the reigns of Felipe III and Felipe IV was accompanied by an unfaltering adherence to the principle of monarchical absolutism. In this period of economic decline and uninspired leadership the Spanish people found consolation for the loss of its preeminence in the idealized picture of national history and customs contained in the Spanish Golden Age *comedia*. [4]

Lope de Vega, the creator of the national Spanish theater, and an artist highly responsive to popular preferences, reflects this monarchical sentiment in his dramas. A study of Lope's King Pedro plays reveals a decidedly seventeenth-century concept of royal power and prerogatives which contrasts sharply with Spanish medieval political theory. Lope's king is surrounded by an aura of semi-divinity which inspires awe in onlookers.

The peasant Bras in *La carbonera* exclaims as he gazes at Pedro de Castilla: «Qué majestad tan temida;/ ¡Retrátese Dios allí!» (II, ix). Another rustic character in *El rey don Pedro en Madrid* has a similar reaction: «Confusión pone el miralle/ Y respecto causa el velle.» (III, xxi). Even the haughty Infanzón Tello García is humbled by the presence of Pedro and admits that he fears the king: «Esta majestad que ves,/ Es la que los hombres tiembla:» (II, xv). The aura of his royal Majesty is manifest even when the

---

[3]   John Neville Figgis, *The Divine Right of Kings* (New York: Harper and Row, 1965), pp. 5-6.
[4]   See Victor Whitehouse, «The Theory of the Divine Right of Kings in the Spanish Drama of the Golden Age» (Unpublished doctoral dissertation, Harvard University, 1929).

king is in disguise, talking a peasant in *Ya anda la de Mazagatos*: «Su severa/ Presencia me maravilla.» (I, xxi).

Lope's king rules by Divine Right. In the *Audiencias del rey don Pedro* King Pedro remarks: «Legítimo rey me hizo el cielo.» (I, viii). Confident of his divine sanction to rule, he fears no opponent: «Y si Dios está conmigo,/ Ni a Enrique ni al francés temo.» (I, viii). The nobleman Jacinto in *El médico de su honra* states clearly the principle of the Divine Right of Kings: «Demás que los reyes son/ Vicedioses en la tierra,/ En que la deidad se encierra.» (I, xiii). Since he is God's representative on earth, the king commands the unquestioning obedience of his subjects. We again see this concept in Lope's *La carbonera*: «Porque es la ley más justa de las leyes,/ Callar, servir y obedecer los reyes.» (I, i).

Ironically, it is the future fratricide Enrique de Trastamara in *El rey don Pedro en Madrid* who makes a series of statements in support of his brother's position as King of Castilla (III, vii). He states that non-resistance and passive obedience to the monarch are religious obligations of the Christian: «Y el que lo llega a culpar,/ Casi pone en Dios defecto.» The king is but an instrument of God's justice. Resistance even to a tyrant is thus a sin so long as it God's will that he continue to rule: «Que es deidad el rey más malo,/ En que Dios se ha de adorar.»

The king's justice, like divine justice, must at times be so swift and severe as to appear cruel: «Y es tal vez justo castigo/ Lo que parece crueldad.» A severe king may be set over a sinful people in order to dispense divine justice most effectively: «Premio y castigo en la ley/ Del rey a un reino se da.» Since the ways of God are inscrutable to man, the people must not question the workings of His justice as administered by His earthly representative: «Y en su execución será/ Sólo el instrumento el rey.»

Lope states in *Ya anda la de Mazagatos* that just as the

king himself may be the only authority to whom a private
citizen may appeal for redress of a tyrannical overlord, so
God is the only authority who may judge and punish a king:
«A la tirana justicia/ Pone Dios leyes y freno.» (II, xxix).
In another passage from *La carbonera* he affirms that it is
God's judgment alone that will accurately assess the perfor-
mance of His earthly representative: «Que de ir contra las
leyes,/ A sólo Dios darán cuenta los reyes.» (III, viii).

Having examined the evolution in Spain of the theory
of Divine Right and its attendant doctrine of non-resistance
to the monarch, we must now investigate the parallel development of the medieval right of resistance. St. Thomas
Aquinas supported the Pauline doctrine of non-resistance
to the sovereign in his *De Regimine Principum*, at the same
time maintaining that one who would usurp the power of
a king may be killed, and that even a legitimate ruler who
degenerated into a tyrant could be deposed by public authority. Spanish Jesuit writers of the sixteenth century
such as Molina, Suárez, Vitoria and Soto reflect the Thomist
view that a Christian should set an example of obedience
and yet not relinquish his right to resist the abuse of power
by a tyrannical ruler. [5]

In his famous treatise *De Rege et Regis Institutione*, [6]
published in 1599, Juan de Mariana shows «an ardent desire
to restore the constitutional tradition of the Middle Ages
and especially the medieval constitution of Spain.» [7] Although he differs from other Jesuit writers of his day in

---

[5]   See Bernice Hamilton, *Political Thought in Sixteenth-Century
Spain* (Oxford: The Clarendon Press, 1963).

[6]   References to this work of Mariana will be taken from the
Spanish translation *Del rey y de la institución real*, *Biblioteca de
autores españoles*, XXI (Madrid: Sucesores de Hernando, 1909).

[7]   Guenter Lewy, *Constitutionalism and Statecraft during the
Golden Age of Spain*: *A Study of the Political Philosophy* of Juan
de Mariana, S. J., Travaux D'Humanisme et Renaissance, XXXVI
(Geneva: Librairie E. Droz, 1960), p. 162.

his insistence upon the necessity of a return to the medieval Spanish *Cortes*, Mariana is strongly in favor of the institution of monarchy, believing it to be the best possible
form of government. Nowhere in the treatise does he
advocate the establishment in Spain of a republic. He
prefers monarchy to other forms of government because,
aside from being more efficient, it conforms best to the
laws of nature. [8] He regards as ideal a monarchy wherein
the king calls together the citizens for their advice and
opinions before taking action [9].

Mariana supports the principle of hereditary right, stating that an orderly succession prevents the civil disorder
that results from the feuding of rivals. A king who knows
that his son will reap the benefits of his good administration
will be less self-seeking. A prince who, while having before him his father's good example, has received an education in the obligations and responsibilities as well as the
rights of kingship, will be less likely to degenerate into self-
indulgence and tyranny than one risen suddenly from a
more lowly state. [10]

Mariana distinguishes between two types of tyrants:
the legitimate ruler who degenerates into a despot, and the
usurper. The latter is an outlaw and may be killed by
anyone. The legitimate ruler who abuses his power may
be admonished by a public assembly of the subjects. If
he chooses to ignore this warning and continues to rule
tyrannically, then the people may depose and even kill
him. Mariana does not say that any private citizen has the
right to take upon himself the killing of a legitimate ruler,
even though he be a tyrant, unless «le pregone como tal

---

[8]   Mariana, pp. 467-471.
[9]   Mariana, p. 472.
[10] Mariana, p. 474,

la fama pública y sean del mismo parecer los varones gra-
ves y eruditos.» [11]

Lope de Vega's plays contain none of Mariana's constitutionalism. As one writer has stated: «Lope saw human
election of kings as an expression of the divine will.» [12]
This concept of popular election does not consider the
people as the source of political authority, but rather as
the instrument through which God, the true source of political power, is intervening in earthly affairs. Although
God's will with respect to a tyrant may be made known to
and executed by the people, this is not to be confused in
any way with the concept of popular sovereignty.

Whereas Mariana uses Pedro de Castilla as proof of
precedent in Spanish history for the right of resistance to
a tyrant, [13] in *Los Ramírez de Arellano*, when Lope shows
the Castilian people supporting the claim of Enrique de
Trastamara against their legitimate ruler Pedro I, the poet
is careful to demonstrate that it is God's will speaking
through people and not a spontaneous expression of the
right of resistance. In this play Lope shows that the king
may be above positive law, but he is bound by Natural Law.
The dramatic character Pedro IV de Aragón is clearly referring to positive law when he says: «El gusto del Rey
es ley.» (II, viii).

On the other hand, the major protagonist Juan Ramírez
refers to Natural Law when he states that his first obligation
is to a law higher than the king: «La ley es lo principal,/
Luego el Rey...» (I, iii). King Pedro has incurred the
wrath of God by his violation of Natural Law, and since he

---

[11] Mariana, p. 483.
[12] Philip Rovner, «Lope de Vega on Kingship» (Unpublished
doctoral dissertation. University of Maryland, 1958), pp. 244-245.
[13] Mariana, p. 481.

persists in defying the higher law of God, he must be deposed:

> Y pues Pedro no se enmienda
> Ni quiere acortar la rienda
> A la crueldad y ambición,
> Dios dará la posesión
> A quien servirle pretenda. (III, i).

Divine sanction of Enrique's claim is therefore inferred. Lope ends the play with an unceremonious report of the death of Pedro, and all present declare vociferously in favor of Enrique II, the new King of Castilla.

Los Ramírez de Arellano is the only play of Lope in which the actual downfall and death of Pedro I are treated, and the king is presented on this occasion as divested of his aura of semi-divinity and is more an object of pity than of censure. Pedro appears only in Act III, and is in reality a rather minor character in the drama. Lope might well have chosen not to have him appear on stage at all, since the scenes in which he appears do not further the action of the plot.

The fact that this genealogical play has as its purpose the idealization of Juan Ramírez de Arellano, a follower of Enrique de Trastamara, makes it necessary that Lope present the cause of the usurper as a just one. This necessitates his presentation of the legitimate ruler King Pedro as a man unfit to rule who has lost his divine sanction and the support of his people.

It is interesting to observe that Lope accomplishes this by having characters other than Pedro himself tell of his cruel deeds and his treachery, delaying his entrance until late in the play when, having lost the support of the people, he is, in effect, no longer king. Thus it is not necessary for him to make an excessive show of his alleged cruel nature, and he may appear more sympathetically as a defeated and broken man.

Lope sympathizes with the dejected Pedro as a man even if he is not able to explain or to justify the severity of his actions as king. In this play the poet presents Pedro as a once proud and aggressive king who has degenerated into a tyrant guilty of desperate and arbitrary deeds.

In addition to creating a many-faceted dramatic character who invites detailed study and analysis by the student of literature, Lope presents in *Los Ramírez de Arellano* an historically verifiable example of the persistence in Spain of the medieval right of resistance of a people against a tyrannical ruler.

CHAPTER III

THE PRUDENT KING AND THE EXEMPLARY MAN

The Pedro of *Audiencias del rey don Pedro* [1] and *Ya anda la de Mazagatos* [2] is a self-possessed and prudent king and a well-intentioned man who has been unjustly maligned because of a misunderstanding of his motives and the misinterpretation of fact. As king he withholds judgment until he has heard all of the evidence in a case, he does not allow

---

[1] This play was first edited in 1899 by Menéndez y Pelayo from a seventeenth-century manuscript. It is contained in Volume IX of the first Academy edition of Lope's works. J. H. Arjona agrees with Morely and Bruerton that this text is not pure Lope in his article «Ten Plays Attributed to Lope de Vega», *Hispanic Review*, XXVIII (October, 1960), 319-340.

[2] This play was not listed among the works of Lope in the bibliography of La Barrera. Lomba y Pedraja was unaware of any extant manuscripts of the play, which he considered to be anonymous. A play by this title is mentioned in several bibliographies and attributed to Lope. One of these bibliographers, Isidoro Fajardo, states that it was included in the *Parte V extravagante de Lope y otros* published in Sevilla. S. Griswold Morley discovered five copies of the play in the Biblioteca Nacional. He prepared an edition of what he believed to be the oldest, indicating the variations found in the other manuscripts. Vern G. Williamsen believes, *La Historia de Mazagatos* to be the earliest version. He states that Lope was not the author of his and certain other plays in the previously missing *Parte XXV extravagante*, which was added to the microfilm collection of the University of Pennsylvania in 1971. See «Lope de Vega: A 'Missing' *Parte* and Two 'Lost' Comedias,» *Bulletin of the Comediantes*, XXV (Fall, 1973), 42-51.

his own emotions to interfere in his decisions, and he tempers his justice with mercy, exhibiting compassion even for those who are clearly in error. As a man he demonstrates patience, courage, a lack of malice, a love of adventure, an appreciation of candor in conversation, and a sentimental affection for the common man and his simple way of life.

Lope presents King Pedro in *Audiencias del rey don Pedro* as both an exemplary man and an exemplary *rey justiciero*. Although the monarch himself mentions his reputation for cruelty, there is in the play no evidence of it in either his words or his actions, and he appears rather as an innocent victim of the ambitions of his bastard brother Enrique.

His brother Tello, who, according to historical evidence was self-seeking and disloyal in his relations with both Pedro and Enrique, is presented as a consistently loyal ally of the king, a fact which, for the purposes of this play, strengthens the presentation of Pedro as the wronged party in the Castilian civil war.

Even before the arrival on stage of King Pedro, Lope sets a mood of sympathy for his plight in the civil war. Diego says: «¡Pobre Rey, que tal ha estado/ Cuatro años en Toro preso.» (I, i). [3] Leonardo agrees: «Que lo siento te confieso;/ Mal Enrique lo ha mirado.» Diego tells of the bastard brothers' treachery during the minority of Pedro and of their imprisonment of him at Toro. Leonardo exclaims: «Le sobra razón/ Para mostrarse indignado/ Contra el Conde.»

Pedro speaks without malice of his brother. His attitude toward Enrique's rebellion is one of bewilderment. When informed that Enrique has been proclaimed king and

---

[3] As we have seen, this period of four years is an historical error which Lope probably took from the account in the *Cuarta Crónica* or from Gratia Dei.

is planning to invade Castilla from France, Pedro, demonstrating courage and self-possession, calmly states: «No temo al Conde, ni del Africano,/ Temor en mi Real pecho no renace.» (I, viii). Pedro states that Enrique will soon earn his reputation as a tyrant and that he will patiently await the advance of Trastamara's forces, secure in the knowledge that the bastard's unjust cause is bound to end in failure.

When, in Act III, Pedro hears that Aragón has broken the peace treaty with Castilla and that Enrique and Bertrand Du Guesclin have crossed into Castilla, Pedro is still confident that God will punish Enrique's presumption:

> Dios los soberbios humilla:
> El es el Señor supremo,
> Su ley católica sigo,
> Y si Dios está conmigo,
> Ni a Enrique ni al Francés temo;
> Que soy cristiano, García,
> Y conozco su poder (III, xvi). [4]

Knowing the facts of Pedro's reign, one might suspect an ironic intent in this speech were the tone not one of such complete seriousness. Nowhere in the play does Lope indicate that he means for the audience to take the words of his character Pedro other than at face value.

---

[4] The tolerance and patience evident in his attitude in this speech is in sharp contrast to the historical accounts, which tell of the bloody vengeance that he took upon even innocent victims who had the misfortune to be relatives of men who had rebelled against him. An example of this is the public execution of Doña Urraca Osorio, the mother of Juan Alfonso de Guzmán. He had escaped Pedro's vengeance by fleeing Sevilla as Pedro was entering the city in 1367. Pedro vented his wrath upon the lady, burning her at the stake. According to a tradition contained in the *Anales* of Ortiz de Zúñiga, a servant of hers, Leonor Dávila, also perished in the flames when she threw herself into the conflagration, carrying a blanket with which to cover the nudity of her mistress, which the fire had exposed.

As a man, Lope's Pedro demostrates gratitude toward his loyal subjects, and a desire to reward their service. In his first appearance in Act I Pedro declares that he is honored by the generous welcome that the city of Sevilla has accorded him, and that once he has ended the rebellion of the bastard brothers he intends to glorify her name and prove that his reputation for cruelty is undeserved. He would like to be able to thank each citizen personally, but the tiresome requirements of official protocol prevent him from becoming too familiar with his subjects: «A no ser a los reyes prohibido/ Y a la Real majestad, que necesita/ De vanos cumplimientos.» (I, viii).

Pedro says that he knows that the noblemen of the city are offended that he has not been to visit them, but that his struggle with his brothers Enrique and Fadrique has made it impossible for him to fulfil his obligations. In this attitude we see a man eager to know his people on a personal level, but who is cognizant of his responsibility to maintain himself aloof as a symbol of royal majesty. He is also aware that he is ruling by Divine Right, and the inexplicable rebellion of Enrique is not only a source of grief to him as a man, but also it is an insult to the very office of the king, and an affront to Divine Authority:

Si legítimo rey me hizo el cielo,
¿Por qué procura el Conde derribarme
Del trono real con avariento celo,
Debiendo, como hermano, acreditarme? (I, viii).

As king, Pedro is conscious of his role as chief law-giver and law-enforcer for his people. Before taking his seat in the first *audiencia* of the play, he makes a statement of his principles as *rey justiciero*:

Rey que delitos abona
Es indigno de ser Rey,
Porque ejecutar la ley
Es conservar la corona (II, x).

He then proceeds to justify his action in putting to death King Bermejo, so that no one may label his deed as cruel. He states that he acted in the matter with the advice of his council. The Maestre de Santiago confirms the justice of the king's procedure, reassuring Pedro of his reputation: «Justicia ha sido, señor,/ Y justamente la fama/ El Justiciero te llama.»

The juxtaposition of Pedro's positive manifestation of zeal for justice and his statement of denial of cruelty underline the apologetic tone which pervades the entire play. Although he is a stern *rey justiciero* in his *audiencias*, Pedro displays compassion for his subjects, and a desire to offer assistance even to those who have by their own errors in judgment brought their misfortune upon themselves.

The first subject to enter the *audiencia* is a *mujer tapada* who claims to have yielded to Leonardo de Maraver only after having received his promise of marriage. Pedro, who upon his arrival in Sevilla had seen this lascivious nobleman and had heard of his reputation, gently reproves the lady for her lack of prudence, reminding her how fragile honor is.

Pedro tells her that the only remedy possible now is for her to plead with Leonardo to marry her, since, there being in reality no broken vow, there are no grounds for his official intervention. Although he seems to be in sympathy with her and he does not condemn her too severely for her error, neither does he agree to take unwarranted official action. He merely reminds her of the seriousness of her situation, and gives her what little advice he can offer.

The second subject to appear in the *audiencia* is a soldier who had lost an arm in a battle in Jaén between the forces of Pedro and those of King Bermejo. He had escaped death only by fleeing the battlefield. He has come to Pedro seeking some compensation for the loss of his arm in the king's service. As in the previous case

of the *mujer tapada* his request is not a legitimate one,
and Pedro severely reprimands him, telling him to go and
join the beggars at the door of a church and to consider
himself fortunate that he is showing this degree of mercy
toward him after hearing of his treachery in deserting his
king on the field of bettle.

Pedro's less compassionate attitude toward this man is
understandable in view of the presumption of his request.
As a traitor, he deserves to die rather than to be rewarded.
Pedro shows tolerance of the man's failings, since he personally despises any demonstration of cowardice: «Siempre/
Los cobardes aborrezco.» [5] Mercy and compassion are
evident in his decision, since he allows the man to live, considering the degradation of his becoming a beggar the most
suitable punishment.

The next subject who attends the *audiencia* is an old
leñador, Pedro Rubio, who had found a purse containing
fifty *doblas marroquíes* and had attempted to return it
to the merchant who had lost it in return for ten *doblas*
which the latter was offering as reward. The merchant
was treacherously accusing him of having stolen ten *doblas*
of the original sixty supposedly contained in the purse.
As soon as he sees Pedro «el justiciero», the distraught
leñador, anticipating just treatment, expresses his relief:
«El temor pierdo.»

Pedro realizes that the devious merchant had repented
of his offer of reward and was trying to avoid having to
repay the honesty of the good Pedro Rubio. He resolves
the conflict by saying that the purse found by the *leñador*
cannot possibly be the one lost by the merchant, since
it contains only fifty *doblas*. He tells Pedro Rubio to
keep the purse, and if he should find one containing sixty

---

[5] Historians agree that the historical Pedro was a courageous
soldier and a skillful military leader. Ayala states that «Fue muy
trabajador en guerra.» (*Crónica*, p. 393.)

doblas, he should immediately contact the merchant. The merchant recognizes the astuteness of the king's decision: «Justamente me castiga.» [6]

In the second *audiencia*, Marcelino, a *zapatero*, appeals to Pedro for justice, protesting the violation of his wife by a *prebendado*. The Archbishop had decreed a light sentence for such a grave offense: that the priest not say mass for six months. The *zapatero* had then taken matters into his own hands and killed the *prebendado*. He had escaped, and, confident of a just decision, he is bringing his case before the king. Pedro demonstrates the incongruity of the prelate's decision by observing ironically «bien juzgó», and he proceeds to decree an equal sentence for the crime of the *zapatero*: that he not make shoes for six months. [7]

Laurencia is the next subject in the second *audiencia* of the play. She brings with her the dagger covered with the blood of Leonardo, whom she had killed in the defense of her honor. Pedro is reminded of a prophetic dream that he had the night before in which Enrique had held such a dagger, threatening his life at Montiel. He dismisses the vision with the vain hope that «los sueños, sueños son». In this play Pedro has a clear conscience, and he is secure

---

[6]   This popular tradition may be found in the *Libro de los enxemplos* and in the *Disciplina clericalis* of Pedro Alfonso. Menéndez y Pelayo notes that this and other legends have also been attributed to Pedro de Portugal, who also had some fame as a *rey justiciero*. Emily Schons suggests that this story may be of Italian origin. She notes also that in the *Floresta española* of Melchor de Santa Cruz there is another version dating from 1574 which contains the same verdict but which differs in some details.

[7]   This popular legend is included in the *Anales eclesiásticos y seculares de la ciudad de Sevilla* for the year 1354. Ortiz de Zúñiga records a new clause added by Pedro I to a law of 1351 which concerns the propriety of vengeance of the common man against crimes of priests when ecclesiastical authorities do not decree appropriate penalties. He directs his *alcaldes* to mete out equal punishment to the private citizen if the one received by the priest is too lenient. The king adds that this law is not intended as an attack upon the power of ecclesiastical authority.

in the knowledge of his rightful possession of the throne. He is not, therefore, distracted from his duties by apparently meaningless omens.

Throughout the play *Audiencias del rey don Pedro* Pedro has maintained his confidence and self-control and has shown himself to be an exemplary *rey justiciero*. The introduction of the disturbing element of the omen foretelling of his death at Montiel, an historical fact which could not be ignored, may have been intended to heighten the irony of his reputation as a cruel tyrant. On the other hand, since the only extant manuscript of the play shows definite signs of having been altered, it is entirely possible that this detail may have been added by another playwright or an *autor de comedias*.

In any event, the tone of the entire play is apologetic to Pedro. Enrique does not appear on stage, and is spoken of in consistently unflattering terms. In the opinion of this writer, there is no reason to suspect that the original author had any purpose other than that of enhancing the reputation of Pedro I as a just and prudent king.

In *Ya anda la de Mazagatos* King Pedro is able to exhibit more sides of his personality than the king of the *Audiencias* because of the fact that he appears in disguise in the first act and is therefore not compelled to maintain the decorous distance required between the representative of his royal Majesty and the common man. In his disguise as a mere nobleman of the court he is free to engage in familiar conversation with his subjects and may express his own opinions as a man.

A favorite pastime of the historical Pedro was that of hunting. [8] In this play this activity is used to bring him into contact with the common people. Since he is clothed in the hunting garb common to all noblemen, and

---

[8]   See Ayala, *Crónica*, p. 593.

the country folk have never seen him in person, they do not know that they are speaking with their king. This gives Pedro an excellent opportunity to investigate the opinions of his people concerning himself and his management of the affairs of the realm.

The plot complications in *Ya anda la de Mazagatos* hinge on the fact that there are two Elviras. One, the daughter of Alvaro and the sister of Juan, has secretly received Manrique as her husband. One night when he is visiting her, they are surprised by the father and the brother. Manrique struggles with Juan, who tears the *escudo* from his cape. Before they can take her to a convent, Elvira escapes and finds refuge in nearby Mazagatos with the family of the second character named Elvira. The rustic Elvira, who is betrothed to Pascual, is also the object of the attentions of the disguised King Pedro, who enjoys the family's hospitality while taking refuge from a storm which has separated him from his hunting party.

Manrique decides to kidnap the rustic Elvira, unaware that the lady Elvira and the king are in the very house from which he intends to take her. Manrique and King Pedro struggle in the dark, and the latter exchanges capes with him in hopes that he may thereby discover the identity of his valiant adversary. The king's possession of the cape from which *escudo* was torn, and confusion of the two separate nocturnal incidents concerning two different Elviras lead to numerous complications of plot.

When Nuño meets what he believes to be one of the royal courtiers who had become separated from the company of the king while hunting near Mazagatos, he offers him refuge for the night from an approaching storm. Although he does not recognize his guest to be the king, he is strangely awed by his presence: «Su severa/ Presencia me maravilla.» (II, ix). When Nuño apologizes for the humble meal, Pedro, as a man, expresses relief at having a brief respite from the rigid protocol of his life at court: «Esta quietud no es mal plato,/ Que el espléndido aparato/ Cansa a veces.» (I, xxiv).

Nuño shows that, although he is a man of humble origin, he is also a man of honor and dignity, aware of the protocol to be observed in social situations, when he objects to his noble guest's not having seated himself in the place of honor. His daughter Elvira, however, demonstrates the lack of necessity for such formality when men are enjoying each other's company as individuals. Her words are laden with dramatic irony when she states that: «Aun el Rey puede cenar/ En mesa de un labrador,/ Si es limpia y está con gana.»

Pedro is thoroughly enjoying the relaxed atmosphere of the dinner conversation. As a man, he is attracted by the beauty of the rustic Elvira and he begins to compliment her in courtly language. Nuño informs his guest that, as head of the household, he does not consider such artificiality appropriate outside of the court. King Pedro respects the caution of Nuño and he does not press his attentions on Elvira.

Nuño speculates upon what the king might be doing. The disguised lady Elvira, who has recognized King Pedro, observes ironically that the king is probably gazing at some lovely peasant girl: «Que el rey también se enamora,/ Como los hombres. (I, xxv). Pedro, in an aside, admits to his amorous nature as a man: «En mí dices la verdad.» [9]

Nuño candidly discusses with his guest his personal disapproval of the king's habit of hunting. Nuño has served as a soldier, and he considers such a frivolous pastime unworthy of a leader in war. Pedro defends the strategy and the rigors of the hunt as being good exercise in times

---

[9] The historical Pedro pursued many females in his lifetime. Ayala states that «amó mucho mujeres.» (*Crónica*, p. 593.)

of peace for those who must maintain their strength and resourcefulness for success in battle.

When the meal is completed and the family is preparing to retire, Pedro reflects upon the day's activities, and he expresses satisfaction at the welcome diversion from his heavy responsibilities and the opportunity to enjoy the company of so lovely a girl as Elvira.

When he sees the shapes of two men in the darkness outside of the house, Pedro supposes them to be two peasants who have come to talk at the *reja* with Elvira. The disguised Manrique, who has come to kidnap Elvira, mistakes the king for his rival Pascual, and he engages him in a duel. Pedro and Manrique are each amazed at the skill and courage of his unknown opponent, and they marvel at the demonstration of such noble *brío* by a peasant. Pedro, as a man, is deeply disturbed at not having been able to defeat the intruder: «Un abismo/ Tengo en el pecho al mirar/ De este rústico lo altivo.» (I, xxvii). Determined to discover his identity, he exchanges capes with him.

As Act II opens, Pedro is restless and he tells his men to make arrangements for the hunt. He is preoccupied with his desire to know the identity of the wearer of the cape, which he has recognized as being the kind worn by noblemen: «¡Curiosos celos me mueven!». Gutierre states that he intends to stay closer to the king on future hunting excursions so that Pedro may be spared a repetition of the disturbing experience. Pedro, on the other hand, demonstrates that he has no regrets concerning the incident:

> Es curiosidad alegre
> De la inclinación real,
> Y suceden accidentes
> Raras veces sucedidos,
> Y más si la noche viene (II, i).

As we shall see, this enjoyment of nocturnal adventure is evident in other King Pedro plays of Lope in which

Pedro habitually disguises himself and wanders about the streets of the city at night.

The king tells Gutierre to go to Mazagatos and paint a portrait of the rustic Elvira so that he may have a remembrance of their meeting. He describes the little village with sentimental affection:

> Esa aldea es Mazagatos;
> Los humos que dejan verse,
> Son de sus humildes casas;
> Las torres y chapiteles
> Bien se divisan, y en ella,
> Por hija, un villano tiene
> A un ángel; llámese Elvira (II, i).

Pedro, who appears in his official role as king throughout the rest of the play, is faced with a difficult situation which will test his patience and self-possession to the limit when Alvaro and Juan come to him to plead justice in the supposed kidnap of the lady Elvira by Manrique. Pedro forces the two men to wait while he engages in the hunting of an elusive deer. This poorly-motivated exit of Pedro is necessary to the plot, since it gives Alvaro and Juan the opportunity to examine the cape and arrive at the mistaken conclusion that the nocturnal visitor to their home was none other than the king himself.

This scene, although loosely constructed, is valuable in that it creates a contrast of character between Pedro and the noblemen Alvaro and Juan. Alvaro complains petulantly of having to wait:

> ¿Es posible que don Pedro
> Por tirar a un gamo deje
> De escuchar nuestros agravios?
> ¡Es cruel y no los siente! (II, ii).

These words, rather than being a legitimate indictment of the king's lack of consideration. demonstrate Alvaro's impatience and his inflated sense of his own importance. In fact, Pedro is unusually patient with Alvaro and Juan in spite of their daring accusations that he has brought dishonor on their name.

Pedro repeatedly pleads with the men to state their grievance in clear terms. Alvaro says that he is reluctant to speak of his dishonor in order to avoid increasing it. This is, of course, not a valid reason for him to withhold information from the king, since there is no one present except for the king and the two injured parties, Alvaro and Juan. By refusing to clarify the details of the situation, Alvaro is prejudicing his own case. The justice of the king is his only hope.

The mistrust of Pedro shown by Alvaro and Juan is most unbecoming behavior in men of noble rank, and would be reason enough in itself for Pedro to punish them severely. Instead, he endures their insolence, attempting to discover the truth in order te be able to act justly in the defense of their honor.

The imprudence of the father and son in speaking in vague terms about their nocturnal visitor and in not giving full details about the cape causes Pedro to come to the mistaken conclusion that they are referring to the episode at Nuño's house, and that it was Juan with whom he had fought. Pedro cannot understand why two noblemen would be interested in the honor of a country girl. Confused, he maintains his composure, even when Alvaro utters a most insolent accusation: «Porque soy Alvaro Pérez/ De Guzmán, y eres casado.» (III, iii). [10] Alvaro is behaving in a most imprudent manner, treating the king almost as if he were his equal.

---

[10] The identity of Pedro's wife in this play is not disclosed, since neither Blanca de Borbón nor María de Padilla is mentioned. Historically, Alvaro Pérez de Guzmán was a traitor to Pedro and the husband of María Coronel, who, according to legend, was the object of an attempted seduction by the over-amorous Pedro.

Pedro tolerates the insolence of Alvaro and suppresses his own anger in an attempt to discover further evidence. His patience and tolerance are commendable, and the fact of his zeal for justice is well established, but his royal dignity suffers in the process. When both father and son raise their voices in exclamations of protest against the supposed kidnapping of «Elvira» by Pedro, the king finally reaches the limit of his patience and has them taken into custody.

After having given Alvaro and Juan every opportunity to present him with evidence for their complaints, and having heard nothing more than insolent accusations against his royal person, Pedro terminates the interview, concluding that such conduct in gentlemen of such high social station can only be the result of madness. By considering them to be mad he also avoids the necessity of punishing their open hostility, which in sane men would constitute treason.

In the second act, King Pedro states that he is making a great effort to be a friend to Alvaro, and that he is willing to overlook the latter's offense to his royal person in an effort to help him. Pedro also reveals his concern for his reputation as *justiciero*, and his genuine love for the people:

> Don Alvaro, los monarcas
> Preciados de justicieros,
> A quejas de sus vasallos,
> No vencidos, sino atentos
> Y piadosos han de estar;
> La potencia y el imperio
> No deben ser tiranía;
> La Justicia, con un peso
> Se pinta por la igualdad,
> Y un ojo solo en un cetro
> Pintó el ejipcio, mostrando
> Que uno ha de ser en el reino
> El cuidado y el amor
> Con los vasallos (II, xxviii).

When Alvaro finally tells him about the *escudo* which he believes to have come from the king's own cape, Pedro solemnly swears that he has never seen Alvaro's daughter. He then repeats his offer of help to Alvaro as both king and friend, adding the warning: «Que un rey da satis?ac-ción/ Solamente por sí mismo,/ No a vasallos atrevidos.» Alvaro, relieved of doubt, is full of praise for Pedro: «¡Vivas los años del fénix,/ Ya que en singular extremo/ Es un fénix de justicia!».

Pedro also demonstrates prudence in the scene with Alvaro and Gutierre, the artist who brings with him the portrait which Pedro has requested. Proud of his work, Gutierre takes Alvaro into his confidence and shows him the finished product, which turns out to be a painting of Alvaro's own daughter. When King Pedro enters, Alvaro once again utters grave accusations, and says that his only redress from such a tyrant is a direct appeal to God. Reconsidering his first impulse to have Alvaro and Juan imprisioned once again, Pedro says: «Su propia ignominia quiero/ Que los castigue.» (II, xxxii).

As in the case of the soldier in the *Audiencias*, Pedro shows that he considers the loss of dignity a severe punishment in itself, and he spares the men's lives in spite of their treason. Both father and son are thoroughly confused when the king says that he does not know the lady in Gutierre's portrait.

In Act III, as Alvaro and Juan are awaiting the entrance of Pedro, the latter complains bitterly of the cruelty of the king, believing that he is deceiving them: «¿Cómo ha de haber justicia/ Con quien la ha de observar y no la tiene?» (III, xvi). This attribution of cruelty to the king is made on the basis of a misunderstanding. In reality, Pedro is completely free of the malice which Juan and Alvaro suspect.

Just as the King Pedro of the *Audiencias* was unjustly

maligned because his people did not know all of the facts
concerning his reasons for the killing of King Bermejo,
in this play Pedro is accused of cruelty because two of
his subjects do not know all of the details of his encounter
with the rustic Elvira.   Had Alvaro and Juan told Pedro the
whole truth, they would have been spared the doubts and
suffering that they have been undergoing, and they would
have also spared the king his discomfort and anguish.

Manrique recognized his error in kidnapping the rustic
Elvira, and he knows that the king could very well have him
executed, but he places his confidence in the mercy of Pedro:

> Que aunque la vulgar idea
> Le da el nombre de cruel,
> Justificada sentencia,
> Mejor será retirarme
> Y ponerme en la presencia
> Del Rey, porque de esta suerte
> La malicia desvanezca (III, xi).

With similar confidence in Pedro's mercy and justice,
Nuño restrains Pascual, who is eager to avenge the dishonor
of his bride.   Nuño urges Pascual to speak with the king:
«Su justicia España tiembla.» (III, xiv).

Pedro demonstrates the impartial nature of his justice
when Pascual comes before him protesting Manrique's kidnap of Elvira.   Although Alvaro is inclined to discount the
testimony of the peasant, Pedro will accord it equal weight
with that of a nobleman: «No lo creyera,/ Si a esta gente
sencilla fe no diera.» (III, xviii).

Pedro summons Manrique and, restraining his anger,
he maintains his composure as he reproves him for not
having been in attendance at court.   He asks him what
he has been doing.   When Alvaro and Juan overhear the
confession of Manrique they marvel at the patience of the
king: «Viva infinito/ Un Rey que nos sufrió con bondad mu-
cha.» (III, xix).   The wisdom of the following words of Man-

rique dramatically demonstrates the lack of prudence of the
father and son: «A los reyes, señor, no ha de negarse/ La
más secreta culpa.» Pedro confronts Alvaro with his error
and reminds him that the king is ever a source of honor
and justice for his subjects:

> Siendo fuente, siendo origen
> Los príncipes y los reyes
> De la justicia y las leyes
> Que en paz a los hombres rigen,
> No se ha de pensar que afligen
> A sus vasallos. (III, xxi).

Pedro exercises both patience and clemency in the case
of Manrique. When Alvaro asks the king to pardon him
so that he may fulfil his promise of marriage to his daughter
Elvira, Pedro agrees to do so, although he states that Manrique's imprudent behavior is deserving of severe punishment. When the rustic Elvira is brought to him and Manrique says that she is not the one whom he had sworn to
marry, the angry and confused king has him imprisoned.

The appearance of the lady Elvira to complain of her
treatment by Manrique increases the king's anger, but he
does not allow his passion to color his judgment. Carefully allowing for the possibility of error, Pedro says to Manrique: «O te engañas, o me engañas.» (III, xxvii).

The people of Mazagatos come to protest Manrique's dis-
ruption of the wedding. Pedro warns Manrique of the
danger of his position: «Contra ti piden venganza/ Muchos,
Conde; preveníos,/ Que soy Rey, y debo darla.» (III, xxviii).
The solemnity and necessity of the king's judgment are
emphasized by the thrice-repeated statement, «El Rey guar-
dará justicia,» which is pronounced first by Nuño, then
the rustic Elvira, and finally by another peasant girl named
Teresa, as they exit one by one.

After Manrique confesses his obligation to the lady El-

vira, Pedro says that he must die for his crime. Alvaro
and both the lady and the rustic Elvira plead for clemency.
Pedro, as a man, is once again attracted by the charms of
the rustic Elvira, and it is her plea which convinces him
to release Manrique. Pedro's attraction to Elvira has remained throughout the play a gentle emotion free of lust or
dishonest intentions, and more reminiscent of the sentimental infatuation of an adolescent boy than the passion
of a full-grown man.

Since she is so closely identified with the village of
Mazagatos and its simple, unspoiled way of life, the king's
affection for Elvira may be viewed as representing on a
small scale his love for all of the common people of his
realm, for whom he feels a deep sympathy in their suffering
and whom he secretly envies because of their uncomplicat-
ed existence.

The King Pedro of *Ya anda la de Mazagatos* exhibits
exemplary qualities both as man and as king. As a man,
he is courageous, adventure-loving, candid, tolerant and
patient. As a king, he is prudent, compassionate, impartial,
and totally committed to his role as a source of honor and
justice for his people.

CHAPTER IV

THE EVOLUTION OF PARANOIA IN LOPE'S KING PEDRO

Unlike the Pedro of the *Audiencias* and *Ya anda la de Mazagatos*, the king of *La niña de plata* and *El médico de su honra* is not successful in restraining his emotions, even when acting in his official position; a fact which results in a serious error in judgment on his part in both plays. An examination of the situations in which his lack of self-control is evident reveals the fact that in each case it results from a disappointment, real or imagined, which he has suffered in his relationship with his brother Enrique.

Lope's King Pedro displays a genuine affection for his brother, and although his devotion to Enrique is an admirable trait in the character of the man Pedro, the actions which he undertakes to prove his brotherly loyalty are to the detriment of his position as king. Repeated disappointments breed a growing fear and suspicion of Enrique on the part of Pedro, who physically assaults his brother in a prophetic scene in *El médico de su honra*.

The King Pedro of *El médico de su honra* is a far more admirable character than is the devious plotter of the *comedia de enredo*, *La niña de plata*. In *El médico de su honra* Pedro demonstrates a desire to know the true opinions of his people concerning him, and he fulfils his role as an exemplary *rey justiciero*. His relationship with Enrique is of particular interest in this play, since we may observe dramatic evidence of the mounting pressures that will eventually lead to the estrangement of the brothers.

Pedro is blind to his brother's lack of respect for the honor of the nobleman Jacinto. The king's failure to realize the fact and to restrain Enrique's rash courtship of a married woman results in a domestic tragedy which might otherwise have been avoided. Pedro's failure to assess accurately Enrique's faults and his overconfidence in the nobility of character of his brother result in a climactic scene in which he becomes so enraged at Enrique's irresponsibility that he resorts to violence and places his own life in danger, a fact which threatens the very stability of his kingdom, since his violent death would result in political chaos.

In *La niña de plata* Lope allows Enrique to shine as the more noble character, depicting Pedro, for all his brotherly devotion, as no more than a proud and quick-tempered man, eager to prove his manly prowess and contemptuous of what he considers any display of weakness on the part of another. There are no scenes involving the *rey justiciero* in the play, and Pedro appears with all the faults of his character as a man and none of the redeeming virtues of the king which we observed in the *Audiencias del rey don Pedro* and *Ya anda la de Mazagatos*.

In *La niña de plata* Pedro is worried about Enrique's depression resulting from an unrequited passion for a lady. He engages in petty and devious intrigue which is beneath the dignity of the King of Castilla. Having vented his frustration at a supposed lack of valor on the part of Enrique, a situation which is the result of a mistaken and trivial matter, the king then feels that he must come to the defense of his brother's position as royal prince. Pedro imprudently loses his temper with a loyal nobleman who declines an honor which Enrique has offered him. This overreaction to a supposed insult demonstrates in dramatic fashion King Pedro's progressive loss of self-control and sound judgment.

In *La niña de plata* the brothers Pedro, Enrique and Fadrique are presented as close friends and constant companions,, and there is no evidence in the scenes in which they appear together of any serious friction between them. In spite of this fact, Lope inserts a discussion between the «niña,» Dorotea, and her aunt Teodora which suggests that there is, in fact, a conflict, although it is not apparent in the dramatic action. Teodora considers this conflict the reason behind Pedro's reputation for severity. Dorotea agrees, adding that Pedro has just cause for suspicion of his half-brothers:

> Como no son de su madre,
> Sino de sólo su padre,
> Pareceránle tiranos
> De las honras que les dio
> Y los estados que tienen. (I, i).

Teodora states that she even suspects that King Pedro may be jealous of his brother Enrique.

As Enrique enters Sevilla he is amazed at the beauty of the ladies who come out on their balconies to welcome him. He asks the nobleman Arias to tell him the names of each as they pass by their houses. Enrique is especially attracted to Dorotea, who is a lady of intelligence as well as beauty. He bribes a squire of the household to arrange for him to visit Dorotea that evening.

Enrique also has Dorotea's brother Félix brought to him, and when he hears that the family is too poor to offer a proper dowry for Dorotea, he sees an opportunity to show an interest in her without arousing the brother's suspicions.

He pretends to commiserate with him in his noble poverty, saying that these are matters «A que debe acudir el justo príncipe.» (I, xii). The irony of this speech is increased when Enrique asks the unsuspecting Félix the name of his sister. When asked later the reason for such deceptive behavior, the Infante rather cold-bloodedly replies: «Junto materiales/ Para aqueste edificio de mi gusto.»

Although Pedro's choleric temperament is commented upon by the nobleman Arias, there is no evidence of it in either his words or his actions in the first scene in which he appears, which shows the three brothers on a nocturnal *ronda* while the city is gay with the celebration of a *fiesta*. King Pedro, Enrique and Fadrique dismount at door of Dorotea's house and ask for water to assuage their thirst. There is an obvious intention of «doble sentido» with the charms of Dorotea, which would quench Enrique's passion.

Pedro is also attracted by the beauty of Dorotea. When Fadrique tells him that Enrique has fallen in love with her, Pedro is amazed at such a sudden show of passion, although he, as a man, can appreciate the worth of its object. Pedro notices that Dorotea does not seem to welcome Enrique's attentions, and he decides to aid his brother in his pursuit of the lady.

Of the three brothers Enrique appears to be the most dashing and attractive as a man. [1] Dorotea admits that she finds Enrique the most appealing, although she diplomatically compliments all three brothers when asked directly by the king which she would prefer as a suitor. This scene was witnessed by Juan, the impoverished nobleman who wants to marry Dorotea, and his jealousy is aroused by the attentions of the Infante. Dorotea assures Juan that she

----

[1] Historical accounts attest to the greater physical attractiveness of Pedro, who was taller and more handsome than Enrique. See Ayala, *Crónica*, p. 593.

has no interest in Enrique, although he is attractive and she is flattered by his admiration of her .

When Pedro hears from Fadrique of the loss of sleep and the extreme depression that Enrique is suffering as a result of Dorotea's scorn, he is concerned for his brother's welfare and he resolves to intervene personally and cure his brother's affliction by having the girl brought to him: «Que viva Enrique, á quien tan mal gobierna/ La razón natural de su albedrío.» (II, vi).

It is at this point in the dramatic action that Pedro makes an error in judgment as king. As we observed in the *Audiencias*, his official position demands that he remain aloof and not deal on a familiar level with his subjects. Although he is making an unselfish effort to assist his brother by enacting this plan, he is also diminishing his official stature by choosing, as a man, to participate directly in the *enredo*.

The fact that Pedro is fully aware of this lack of decorum on his part is demonstrated clearly throughout the scenes in which he discusses the action he plans to take and when he goes in person in the company of Fadrique and Arias to put the plan into action.

Pedro tells Arias to take a thousand *escudos* and two valuable golden chains with him to Dorotea's house in an effort to win her favor. In this scene, Pedro assumes the role of an older and wiser man in affairs of the heart who will employ his own knowledge and personal resources to aid the pretensions of his less experienced brother. He sympathizes with him, and he resolves to put an end to his melancholy by the use of a bribe.

When Pedro arrives with Fadrique and Arias to effect the plan, they become aware of the presence of other men in the street. Not to be outdone by his brother Fadrique, Pedro proves that he is a man of action and courage:

> Pues yo os prometo
> Que aunque soy rey y reservarme es justo,
> Que me saben tan bien seis cuchilladas
> Como al bravo mejor de aquesta tierra. (II, xv).

Pedro has admitted that such bravado is not becoming to his position as king, but the assertion of his personal courage as an individual man is so important to him that he will risk the loss of decorum. He seems pleased when Arias affirms his reputation for courage and skill: «Más quisiera topar con treinta bravos/ Que á Vuestra Majestad sin conocerle.»

When the prearranged signal is given for the lady to come to the door, she is not Dorotea, but Marcela, who is living in the house temporarily. Marcela is flattered by a request for an interview from none other than the king himself. Completely ignorant of Pedro's intentions, and unaware that he believes her to be Dorotea, she leaves the house with him. Juan also believes the *dama tapada* to be Dorotea.

Pedro is disappointed to learn that his plan has failed, and he observes that the bribes were «mal empleadas». He realizes that this abortive effort on his part may have served to increase the affliction of Enrique. When Arias suggests the new tactic of enlisting the aid of Dorotea's aunt Teodora, Pedro reaffirms his confidence in the power of a rich bribe in assuring the success of a venture: «No creo/ Que hay imposible al deseo,/ Si lleva plata en la mano.» (III, i). This preoccupation of Pedro with the power of money as a cure-all in dishonorable negotiations also detracts from his high position as king.

Won over by the bribe, Teodora speaks with Enrique, who demonstrates the debilitating effect that his passion has had on him: «Estoyme muriendo;/ No duermo, como, ni vivo» (III, iii). He is so enamored of Dorotea that he has allowed his preoccupation with her to cause him to place his love for her above the welfare of his own brother the king. Enrique reveals in this scene that he has no illusions concerning marriage to Dorotea. [2] Assured entry into her bedchamber, Enrique resolves to take her by force if necessary.

Once he is face-to-face with Dorotea, however, Enrique's nobility of character prevents him from carrying out his base intentions. Her profession of love for Juan and her resolution to commit suicide if dishonored temper his passion, if they do not diminish his original attraction to her. He promises to arrange personally her marriage to Juan, and he states that he is confident that his actions will win him renown as «el cortés galán».

When Enrique speaks to Juan's greedy father, the *veinticuatro*, he tells him that he will provide a rich dowry if Juan is allowed to marry Dorotea. The old man is delighted at the prospect of both wealth and the acquisition of membership in the Order of Santiago. His glee is curtailed when Juan tells him that he had seen Enrique enter Dorotea's room after dark. The father resolves to reject the Infante's offers.

Enrique returns from his interview with the father and tells his brothers Pedro and Fadrique that he has not carried out his intentions with regard to Dorotea. Believing that a lack of valor had been the reason for his restraint, and not allowing Enrique to defend himself against the charge, both brothers reprove him for his supposed weakness. Pedro criticizes his fickle resolution and voices deep disappointment in his brother: «Mucho me ha pesado, Enrique/ Que seas tan para poco.» (III, xii).

After a lengthy tirade on the part of Fadrique concerning the ease with which Enrique could have accomplished

---

[2] There is confusion in Act III of the manuscript in the Biblioteca Nacional of the names Teodora and Dorotea.

his aim, since all obstacles had been removed, Enrique agrees
that he is indeed deserving of a severe reprimand, but not
for lack of courage.   Interrupting him before he can finish
his remarks, Pedro agrees that there is virtue in resisting
one's own passion, but he warns Enrique against attempting
to label as virtue a demonstration of weakness.

When Dorotea arrives, Pedro scornfully asks her to
describe the scene which has resulted in Enrique's shame:

> ¿Cómo fue? ¿Qué sucedió?
> ¿Tembló? ¿Lloró? ¿Tuvo frío?
> Para preciarse de brío,
> Mucho crédito perdió. (III, xiii).

The statement of Dorotea that the brothers should esteem
the Infante for his action is followed by the unexpected
announcement of her intention to marry. Pedro is irritated at not knowing the identity of the groom.   His irritation
and impatience increase as the scene progresses, reaching
a climax when Juan's father arrives and says that he is
refusing the honors that Enrique has offered him.   Confused, frustrated and angry, Pedro allows his passions as
a man to overcome his better judgment, and he forgets
the decorum required by his position as king.

The timing of this announcement by the *veinticuatro*,
coupled with his mounting anger toward his brother Enrique result in a sudden explosion of emotion on the part of
Pedro.   Compelled to defend the very source of a recent
disappointment against an apparent insult on the part of
an outsider, Pedro vents his pent-up wrath upon the new-
comer.   He releases his frustrations by angrily upbraiding
Juan's father: «¡Así los reyes se engañan!» (III, xiv). He
demands to know how the *veinticuatro* could dare to refuse
an honor granted him by a member of the royal family:
«¿No bastaba,/ Para que os viniera bien,/ Ser mi sangre
y vos nada?» He then utters the most irresponsible words

of all, which demonstrate his almost complete loss of self-control and judgment: «¡Vive Dios, que desde aquí/ A los dos en esa plaza/ Han de cortar la cabeza!» Only now does he hear the testimony of Enrique concerning his reasons for restraint with Dorotea.

Lope presents Enrique's victory over himself as a demonstration of his superior nobility of character, and his positive action to restore Dorotea's reputation as a genuine proof of his worth as a man of honor. Once his anger subsides, Pedro agrees to contribute to the dowry. He adds that he and his future queen Blanca will serve as *padrinos* for the wedding.

This generous but tardy action of Pedro is a very weak ending for his character portrayal in the play. In this final scene Enrique has given ample proof of his control over himself. It is obvious that the unfortunate experience has caused him to grow in wisdom and maturity, while at the same time it has provided an occasion for a clear demonstration of a lack of self-control and sane judgment on the part of King Pedro.

Perhaps the root of the problem lies in the fact that Pedro, as a man, places undue importance upon an outward show of physical skill and courage. Had the man in question been other than his own brother he might have been more prudent in his confrontation with him, but since he feels so strongly his position as an older brother, he tends to view Enrique through the eyes of a disappointed parent punishing a younger member of the family for failure to meet the latter's standards.

Pedro's affection for Enrique is apparent throughout the play. His concern for his brother's suffering causes him to enlist the aid of the Moor Zulema: «De gran melancolía/ Tengo un hemano enfermo, a quien adoro,/ Y que le cures deste mal querría.» (II, VII). He reveals his willingness to spare no expense in the care of his beloved brother:

«Si un tesoro/ Me cuesta su salud, quiero que quedes/ Del amor que la tengo satisfecho.»

Aside from the evidence of Pedro's own words and actions, we have the confidence that Enrique feels in the king's devotion. When he hears the unexpected prediction of Zulema that he is to flee Castilla for fear of his brother's vengeance, Enrique cries: «¿Qué dices, que adora en mí?» (II, xx). He cannot accept the idea that his own devoted brother will be the murderer of his mother and his brother Fadrique. Neither can he conceive of his own murder of Pedro or of his destiny to be king in his own right. Pedro himself demonstrates the fact that he attaches no importance to fortune-telling: «Juicios para mí son cuentos vanos.» (II, vii). [3]

Pedro also appears as a devoted brother of Enrique in Lope's *El médico de su honra*. In this play Lope presents not only the stern and exemplary figure of Pedro the king, but he also develops the personality of Pedro as a man, demonstrating aspects, such as his sense of humor, which we do not see in the three plays we have discussed so far. One scholar who compares the better-known *refundición* of Calderón de la Barca with Lope's original creation [4] has

---

[3] The historical Pedro's interest in predictions is well known. Ayala includes two letters to Pedro from the Moorish fortune-teller Benahatin. The first letter, which arrives shortly after Pedro's victory at Nájera, contains advice to King Pedro in the form of «exemplos y castigos.» He tells Pedro to love his people, to refrain from cruelty and avarice, to reward loyal service, and to obey his own laws. The second letter arrives just as Pedro is going to the aid of Toledo in 1369, the last year of his reign. This letter contains a prophecy of Merlin in which a bird of prey, once surfeited, loses its wings and its feathers and goes from door to door, seeking assistance. Finding none, it goes into the forest, where it dies twice; once before the world, and once before God. According to the Moor, the bird of prey is Pedro, who will die at Montiel for having violated both human and divine law. Mariana also includes the prophecy of Merlin, and he mentions the Moor Benahatin, whom he calls Benagatin.

[4] Albert E. Sloman considers conclusive proof that Lope's

stated that although Lope's Pedro is presented as more of a *rey justiciero*, he is also cruel, impulsive and quick-tempered. [5]

In the opinion of the present writer, Lope's Pedro is severe rather than cruel, and his quick temper is evident on only one occasion in the play: his last scene with his brother Enrique. While this show of anger results in part from Pedro's desire to protect the honor of Jacinto, who is overhearing the conversation, another reason for Pedro's sudden display of anger lies in his relationship with his brother and is the result of his disappointment in Enrique for not meeting the standards of conduct which Pedro expects of a royal prince.

Criticism has been levelled against Calderón's Pedro for leaving the side of his unconscious brother after his fall from his horse in the first act. [6] In Lope's play, which contains an almost identical scene, the sarcastic observation of the nobleman Pedro: «¡Buena visita de hermano!» is countered by the praise of another nobleman, Alvaro, who lauds Pedro's action as evidence of good judgment: «Su entereza en todas cosas/ El mundo admira.» (I, iv).

A. Irvine Watson observes that these remarks, which

---

play was the source for Calderón's the fact that the ballad «La amiga de Bernal Francés,» which is used for the last scene of Act II of both plays is followed more closely in Lope's version. See his article: «Calderón's *El médico de su honra* and *La amiga de Bernal Francés*,» *Bulletin of Hispanic Studies*, XXIV (1957), 168-169. See also: A. David Kossoff, «*El médico de su honra* and 'La amiga de Bernal Francés*,», *Hispanic Review*, XXIV (1956), 66-70. Calderón changed the names of the husband and wife from Jacinto and Mayor to Gutierre and Mencía, a fact which Menéndez y Pelayo considers to be an influence of Claramente's *Deste agua no beberé*, which also treats King Pedro and has characters with the names Gutierre and Mencía.

[5]   Albert E. Sloman, *The Dramatic Craftsmanship of Calderón* (Oxford: The Dolphin Book Company, 1958), pp. 41-42. See also: C. A. Jones, ed., *El médico de su honra of Calderón de la Barca* (Oxford: The Clarendon Press, 1961), pp. xix-xx.

[6]   Sloman, pp. 41-42.

are similar in Lope's and Calderón's plays, have the dramatic purpose of awakening the audience's interest concerning the character of Pedro, who will reveal qualities of reserve and severity rather than cruelty. Watson continues:

> He is a strong king who refuses to allow himself to be diverted from the path of duty by his personal concern for his brother; he realizes that there is work to be done in Seville, and that it is his solemn duty to place himself at the disposal of his subjects. [7]

In Lope's play Pedro arrives onstage after the accident has taken place, and he dismounts to see what the problem is. The nobleman Pedro observes: «No ha sido fineza poca/ Para su severidad/ Apearse.» (I, iii). Alvaro comments upon the king's resourcefulness: «¿Quién ignora/ Su resolución, midiendo/ Las palabras con las obras?»

It has been stated that Enrique is the only «wilfully evil» character in the play. [8] As we shall see, the realization of Enrique's treachery will be a source of disappointment and even disillusionment for King Pedro.

In the first scene the noblemen Alvaro and Pedro lament the unfortunate accident of the Infante. Alvaro speaks of his «juventud briosa,» while Pedro tells of his «mocedad orgullosa.» Both of these descriptions give the impression that Enrique is a high-spirited and proud young man who has not yet fully matured. Were Mayor still the unmarried girl he had courted earlier, the play would not have the tragic outcome, and Enrique's lack of discretion would have the character of another youthful escapade. However, since he is a royal prince who should know his responsibility to honor the Castilian people, his dishonest

---

[7] A. Irvine Watson, «Peter the Cruel or Peter the Just?» *Romanistisches Jahrbuch*, XIV (1963), 331.
[8] Sloman, p. 41.

designs with regard to a married woman are inexcusable.

The nobleman Pedro expresses his hope that no evil may befall Enrique as a result of the omen of his fall from the horse:

> Ruego al cielo que este agüero
> No anuncie, entre obscuras sombras,
> Que te traen presentes penas,
> Aquellas pasadas glorias. (I, ix).

When Enrique awakens to find Mayor at his side, he is delighted to see her again and he is reminded of the attraction that he had felt for her in the past. Upon hearing that she is now a married women, he tries to rid himself of his desire to press his attentions upon her anew. He refers to the horse which had occasioned this meeting, and he wishes that he had died in the fall. [9]

This second mention of the horse emphasizes the importance of the fall as an omen of Enrique's symbolical «fall» into a passion which will bring suffering to many persons.

Mayor reveals to Elvira the fact that she had married Jacinto in order to assure her honor from the pretensions of the Infante, never imagining that, once in her secure position as a married woman, she might have occasion for further anxiety.

She is astonished and dismayed to recognize Alvaro, who brings the unconscious Infante to her country house after his accident. Mayor tells Enrique that although she had welcomed his attentions while an unmarried woman, she had realized that the two could never marry, and her only desire now is to be allowed to live in peace and honor with her new husband.

---

[9] For a discussion of the fall from a horse as a symbol of one's loss of control over passions, see Angel Valbuena Briones, *Perspectiva crítica de los dramas de Calderón* (Madrid: Rialp, 1965), pp. 35-53.

Jacinto's arrival and his immediate demonstration of
jealousy reinforce the climate of suspicion which had been
created earlier by Mayor's suspicions concerning her husband's absence and by her conversation with Enrique.
This, combined with the omen, prepared the audience for
Enrique's resolution: «Que ahora/ Más facilmente podré/
Gozarla.» (I, vii). Mayor senses immediately the danger
of her situation: «Estoy temerosa,/ Porque soy muy des-
dichada.»

Enrique, feeling better, orders preparations for his return to the city: «Parece que he vuelto en mí» (I, vii).
The use of the verb *parecer* is telling. Since his fall from
the horse and his meeting with Mayor he has undergone a
change from which he will not recover. His reason has
been clouded by a passion which will cause him to disregard his responsibility to Jacinto's honor, and which will
bring about the death of the innocent wife. Jacinto offers
the Infante a fine horse for his return to Sevilla. Enrique's
words are heavily laden with dramatic irony as he thanks
him for the gift and promises to repay his generosity:

> Estimo vuestra persona,
> Don Jacinto; y pues decís
> Las partes de que se adorna
> Ese bruto, yo le acepto,
> Y prometo en otra cosa
> Pagarle. (I, vii).

The «otra cosa» to which he refers will be his treachery
in the destruction of Jacinto's reputation. Jacinto replies
nobly: «Dueño de todo/ Sois, señor.» This speech is also
highly ironical, since Enrique, as a royal prince, has control
over the possessions and even the life of the Castilian people, but he is not the master of Jacinto's honor, which is
the «patrimonio del alma.» As Enrique departs, he says:
«Vamos: mejora/ Amor mi suerte importuna.» Again the

ironic intent of his words is clear. His dishonest passion for Mayor will result not in an increase of good fortune, but rather in his exile from the royal court, the loss of the king's favor, and the destruction of his brother's faith in him.

The presence of Enrique has resulted in a worsening of the already tense marital relationship between Jacinto and Mayor. As he prepares to return to the court in Sevilla, Jacinto expresses, in an aside, his increased anxiety: «¡Qué de laberintos forman/ Mis intricados deseos!» (I, vii). Mayor, also in an aside, reveals her own mounting apprehension: «Mil sospechas temerosas/ Quedan en mi pecho.» On the other hand, Enrique revels in the anticipation of his conquest: «¡Cómo imaginan la gloria/ Mis amorosos deseos/ En su batalla amorosa!»

When he asks Mayor how he may serve her, she replies: «Siempre me honra/ Como quien es Vuestra Alteza.» This reminder of the Infante's responsibility as a symbol of the honor of his people contrats sharply with the base intentions which he has revealed. In this early scene of the play, Lope has set the mood of suspicion which will prevail throughout the drama and he has allowed the character Enrique to demonstrate by his own words the selfishness and irresponsibility which will be the cause of immediate domestic tragedy in the case of Mayor and which will also contribute to the future tragedy of his brother King Pedro.

King Pedro expresses his gratitude to the city of Sevilla for the enthusiastic welcome which he has received and his willingness to honor its citizens for their display of loyalty to him. In this scene Pedro's role as a conscientious *rey justiciero* is firmly established, for as soon as he has uttered his praise of Sevilla, a servant enters to announce the arrival of an aggrieved citizen who is seeking his justice. Pedro directs him to have her enter, demonstrating his desire to be available to all who seek his assistance, and revealing his personal concern for his subjects: «Bueno./ ¿Cuándo de amor estoy lleno/Negáis la puerta? (I, xii). Pedro voices his strong desire to see justice done in these words to Margarita: «Que soy Rey, y justiciero,/ Y hacer justicia espero.» She reassures him of his reputation:

> Rey invicto,
> Que de justiciero nombre
> te dan, digno que la fama
> Lo escriba en hojas de bronce...

As a man, Pedro is attracted by her beauty. This very human display of appreciation for feminine attractiveness has been criticized as detracting from the gravity of Lope's Pedro as a king. One critic goes so far as to state that Lope's Pedro allows his judgment to be swayed by his anger at Jacinto for violating the honor of such a lovely woman, and he praises the more perfect self-control of Calderón's king.[10] In the opinion of the present writer, there is no evidence of this in the king's actions, and she considers this criticism of Lope's dramatic character unwarranted in view of the fact that while in Calderón's play the king serves as a static symbol of authority whose personality as a man is not emphasized, in Lope's version his personality as a man is of extreme importance, and the relationship between the brothers Pedro and Enrique is a major source of conflict in the play which will lead to a loss of self-control on the part of the king later in the play.

Although angered by the treachery of Jacinto, far from allowing his emotion to cloud his judgment, Lope's Pedro proceeds in an exemplary and psychologically shrewd manner to discover the evidence against Jacinto by placing him on the defensive in their interview in order to elicit from

---

[10] Watson, p. 342.

him the most complete testimony. Placed in such an un-comfortable position, and knowing that the king is in full possession of the facts, Jacinto will not be likely to withhold any details which might aid Pedro in arriving at a decision. The two interested parties will thus have been given an equal opportunity to present an impassioned defense.

This technique shows that Lope's Pedro is not content with a purely objective examination of the cold facts, but he is also aware of the importance of delving into the human factors involved in a case in order to assess the degree of malice with which an alleged crime has been committed. By forcing Jacinto to present an impassioned defense of his own actions, he may learn of details which might not otherwise have come to his attention and which will enable him to accord both interested parties impartial considera-tion before arriving at his decision.

It is in the interest of impartial justice that he has Margarita conceal herself and overhear Jacinto's testimony. In this way, Pedro can observe her spontaneous reaction to any new evidence which may come to light in Jacinto's defense.

Genuine affection is evident in the cordial welcome with which Pedro receives his brother Enrique when he arrives in the company of Jacinto. He reveals his concern for Enrique's well-being after his accident: «Púsome en grande cuidado/ Tu caída.» (I, xiii). In contrast to the warm reception which he has shown the Infante, Pedro shuns the noble Jacinto, refusing to allow him to kiss his hand: «Nunca a un villano/ Doy la mano: desviad.» Pedro astutely takes the measure of the man by unexpectedly insulting him and taking careful note of his reaction.

Having heard a severe accusation against Jacinto, the king desires reassurance of the man's personal worth before proceeding to an examination of the evidence against him. He allows Jacinto to complain of the injustice of this rebuff, and to discourse upon the position of the king as God's representative on earth and evil advisers at court, not interrupting him until, his self-pitying at an end, he asserts himself as a man of honor eager to avenge himself upon a slanderer.

Only after Jacinto has thus proved himself to be a man of action and valor does Pedro deign to address him again. When he does, it is with the following words: «Temed, y no me enojéis.» A man of courage himself, Pedro desires to command the respect of his most noble subjects. He is satisfied of Jacinto's personal worth, and he now proceeds to investigate the degree of his guilt in Margarita's dishonor.

He confronts Jacinto with the document signed by him in which he promised to marry the lady. When Jacinto admits that the signature is his, Pedro calmly asks him to explain the reasons for his volation of his word as a gentleman. The concealed Margarita voices her admiration of Pedro's procedure: «¡Oh, qué bien le aprieta agora/ El Rey así!». The seriousness of his loss of the king's favor forces Jacinto to reveal a fact which, were he not in such a defensive position, he probably would not have mentioned in the presence of Enrique and Alvaro: that he had seen another man leaving the house of Margarita one night when he had come to visit her.

Under less pressing conditions, his concern for the lady's reputation would prevent him from telling of this incident within the hearing of anyone other than the king. Had he been less preoccupied with his own defense, Jacinto might have thought to ask to speak with the king in strict privacy before revealing this fact. However, this would have left the audience in doubt as to Margarita's innocence, a problem which is immediately avoided by Alvaro's aside telling of his secret presence at Margarita's house.

The sudden outburst of Jacinto which is occasioned by

Alvaro's admission that he was involved in the incident causes Pedro to have the two men imprisoned for drawing their
swords in the royal presence. In this final scene in Act I
Lope contrasts Pedro's altruistic concern for Margarita with
the selfish and irresponsible preoccupation of Enrique with
the seduction of Mayor. Saddened at having to imprison
two of his loyal subjects, Pedro forgets his own unhappi-
ness and goes to console the aggrieved Margarita.

Enrique, who has remained a silent witness throughout
the entire scene, and who has not seen fit to come to Alvaro's
defense by admitting that he, too, had been present at Margarita's house on the night in question, shows clearly that
he is thinking only of himself and his selfish pleasure:

> Dichoso
> Soy; esta noche, la pena
> Quisiera ¡oh Mayor! volar
> A tu quinta: el cielo ordena
> Mi dicha, pues queda preso
> Don Jacinto en esta torre:
> Mi desdicha el nombre borre
> Con tan extraño suceso. (I, xv).

In Act II when Margarita informs King Pedro that she
plans to enter a convent and she asks him to pardon Jacinto
and Alvaro, there is great irony in Pedro's statement that
his personal inclination would be to force the offender of
her honor to marry her even if he were his own brother
Enrique. The audience is prepared by this statement of resolution on the part of Pedro for his approval as king of
the Infante's self-imposed exile at the end of the play. His
impartial justice demands that he punish all offenders of
the honor code without regard to their rank in the social
hierarchy.

However, Lope has another reason for introducing this
event in the dramatic action. He is demonstrating the fact

that Pedro, as a man, having lost confidence in the nobility
of his brother, has come to suspect his personal loyalty to
him as well, a fact which causes him anguish both as man
and as king.

The trusting attitude which Pedro displays toward Enrique is evident in a brief scene between the brothers in
Act II. Pedro confides in his brother and asks his advice
about his proposed marriage to Blanca de Borbón. Enrique
tells him that he cannot give advice in such a grave matter.
This short verbal exchange between brothers adds another
dimension to the character of Pedro, who reveals himself to
be a prudent and conscientious king, desirous of the well-
being of his people and anxious to give them a worthy queen:

> Porque yo quisiera dar
> Reina tan grande a Sevilla,
> Que fuera, por sus extremos,
> Lo que hoy en Sevilla vemos,
> Una octava maravilla. (II, viii).

The decision is weighing heavily upon his thoughts.
Uncertain, he calls upon Enrique because he is his
half-brother and his close friend, but the final decision must
be made by Pedro alone.

In the brief moment between Pedro's summons of the
two prisoners and their arrival onstage Lope has presented
the lonely position of all kings and heads of state, who may
consult with advisers concerning future actions, but who
bear the full responsibility for all decisions. Lope has also
adeptly demonstrated the complete faith that Pedro has in
Enrique's loyalty and affection toward him, a confidence
which will be destroyed by the end of the play.

Pedro's total confidence in Enrique's nobility of character is the cause for his insistence that Jacinto conceal himself in order to overhear his conversation with his brother
in which he questions him concerning the grave accusation

of Jacinto that the Infante seeks the dishonor of Mayor. Satisfied of the worth of Jacinto, Pedro is anxious to leave no doubts in this nobleman's mind as to the integrity of Enrique.

When Enrique enters, Pedro uses the same technique for establishing the valor and worth of the man which he had employed in the earlier scene with Jacinto. This action is probably as much for the benefit of the concealed Jacinto as it is for his own personal reassurance.

He places his brother immediately on the defensive by calling him a «villano.» However, the result of this investigation comes as a complete surprise to the trusting Pedro. Instead of indignantly denying the charges, Enrique shows that he is indeed guilty of flagrant disrespect for Jacinto's honor. As he tries to tell Pedro of his prior interest in Mayor, Pedro is stunned by the unexpected turn of events which has spoiled his plan for establishing his brother's innocence.

Painfully aware that he has caused an increase of Jacinto's dishonor which he might otherwise have avoided, he interrupts Enrique's testimony with vain attempts to insist upon the impossibility of Mayor's interest in the Infante. He is so angered by the proof of Enrique's lack of nobility of character that he forgets his official position as king and he reacts in a manner similar to the angry brother of *La niña de plata*.

He is desirous of punishing a betrayal of the trust which he had placed in the Infante both as king and brother, while at the same time he is anxious to prevent an increase of the dishonor of the eavesdropper Jacinto. Since he has in his hand the dagger which Jacinto had given him as proof of Enrique's guilt, his physical attack on Enrique involves the possibility of death for both brothers. This lack of prudence is inexcusable in Pedro as king, but it is, perhaps, understandable in Pedro as a man, who feels betrayed by another whom he had always treated with respect and trust.

When he cuts his own hand on the sharp blade, Pedro realizes the serious error that he has made in allowing himself to be carried away by his anger. His words: «¡Oh, qué ciego barbarismo!/ ¡Ya soy de fuego un abismo!» (II, x), may be viewed as reflecting at the same time his dismay at Enrique's blind passion which led to his irresponsible behavior in dishonoring Mayor and to his own irresponsible reaction as a result of his violent anger.

In his blindness to the faults of Enrique Pedro the king has made a serious error. He has allowed his private feelings of affection and trust to destroy the impartiality of his assessment of the Infante as a man. By this misjudgment he has endangered the welfare of the whole kingdom. The safety of the king is absolutely essential to political stability in the realm. Had he been killed in the struggle with Enrique, Castilla would have been subjected to the civil disorder which results from the death of a reigning monarch when there is no clearly designated successor. Enrique would be implicated in his death, and would not be able to become king until he had been cleared of charges of treason.

Pedro minimizes his own injury when Jacinto rushes to his aid, and he takes full responsibility for the violence: «Enojéme agora aquí/ Y el enojo arrojó en mí/ La sangre precipitada.» His immediate concern is for the effect which this scene may have had on Jacinto, and he pleads with him to stay and talk with him as soon as he has stopped the bleeding from his wound. Not until later in the play do we see the effect that this incident has had on Pedro.

In Act III, we learn that although he considers his wound an *agüero*, Pedro does not dwell upon its implications, since he is still full of self-confidence and secure in his position as king, but he does say that he intends to make an increased display of his personal worth. In this scene we hear him make a strong resolution, speaking more as Pedro the man than as King Pedro: «Venceré mi estrella/ Con notable maravilla.» (III, ii).

Although Pedro is not overly concerned about the omen, he does feel that some further action on his part may be necessary to dispel any doubts that others may have concerning his future. He is proud and confident that he will be successful in his attempt. The violent scene with Enrique has resulted in serious doubts concerning the loyalty of his brother. When Alvaro tells Pedro that Enrique plans to leave the city for fear of his brother's vengeance, Pedro replies curtly:

> Váyase de mi presencia;
> Pague su error con ausencia,
> Pues mi presencia ofendida
> Tiene. (III, ii).

No longer does he have confidence in the brother in whom he had confided, and his anger and resentment have increased since the incident.

Pedro's next words are an expression of his intention to go out in disguise that night and «rondar la calle.» He tells Alvaro that he is to accompany him. The timing of this action shows a double purpose in this play. As a man, the ritual of the *ronda* will satisfy his spirit of adventure and help him to rid himself of the frustration of his disagreement with Enrique. As a king, he will have an opportunity to hear his subjects' opinions concerning himself and his actions, a preoccupation which he states clearly in his words to Alvaro:

> El juez más verdadero
> Es, don Alvaro, de un rey,
> Sin eximir de la ley,
> El vulgo terrible y fiero.
> ¡Qué bien delitos relata,
> Qué sin rebozo los dice,
> Qué a su salvo los maldice,

> Y qué sin riesgo los trata!
> Y así, por expresa ley,
> Se había de disfrazar,
> Para poder escuchar
> Su bien o su mal, el rey. (III, vi).[11]

This speech demonstrates Pedro's genuine concern for knowing the truth about himself. His admiration of candor, which we observed in *Ya anda la de Mazagatos*, is once again evident. He is not a king who listens only to the servile flatterers of his court. Unlike the Pedro of *La niña de plata*, he will not be content with the praise of one of his courtiers. Alvaro lauds this characteristic of his king:

> No en balde, señor, te aclaman
> Por Rey justo y por severo,
> Y no en vano el Justiciero,
> Don Pedro, todos te llaman. (III, vi).

Obviously enjoying the anonymity of his disguise on the *ronda*, Pedro pauses to admire a good singing voice:

> Es un atributo santo,
> Que participa de gloria
> Más que humana, pues eleva,
> Siendo agradable y sonora. (III, viii).

This brief episode demonstrates anew Pedro's delight in escaping the heavy responsibilities of his office in order to enjoy the simple pleasures of an ordinary man. When he and Alvaro encounter the barber, Pedro's reaction to his account of Jacinto's vengeance is one of awe and even re-

---

[11] Menéndez y Pelayo states that this is the first instance of which he is aware of the dramatic representation of King Pedro as a «rondador de noche por amor a la justicia». Calderón includes a reference to the *ronda*, but he does not make so clear a statement of its purpose.

spect. He cannot help but admire the «estilo tan noble,» but he is uneasy and shows an almost supertitious dread:

> Fieras congojas
> Asaltan a mis sentidos;
> Entrad dentro: ¡mentirosa
> Salga mi sospecha, amén! (III, ix).

As we can see in the words of Pedro, he is far from an impassive observer and uninvolved judge of the incident. He has been shaken emotionally by the unusual deed. However, as king he must present a serene countenance and, not allowing his own feelings to be visible, he must be the stabilizing influence in the tense and emotionally-charged situation.

Pedro begins by reminding Jacinto of the transitory nature of earthly life. His high praise of the unusual vengeance of Jacinto reflects the opinion of Pedro both as man and as king. Soon after the incident with Enrique he had resolved to make an increased demonstration of his personal worth in order to prove that he is an unusually worthy man as well as an exemplary king. By recognizing the ideal nature of such an extreme example of vengeance, Pedro, in addition to upholding the ideal of the honor code, is also offering the audience insight into the unusual measures which he will employ in order to maintain his position as king.

Lope's King Pedro shows a keen sense of humor in his scenes with the *gracioso* Galindo. [12] He is amused by Galindo's fear when the latter unexpectedly stumbles into the

---

[12] Calderón's King Pedro is more stern with Coquín. A. A. Parker interprets the inclusion of a bargain between the king and the *gracioso* in Calderón's play as an evidence of his cruelty. Coquín will be rewarded if he succeeds in making the king laugh. If he does not succeed, he will have his teeth drawn. Parker concludes that, since king is incapable of laughter, the bargain is both cruel and inhuman and was intended by Calderón to demonstrate the cruelty of Pedro. A. Irvine Watson offers a different interpretation

royal chamber and finds himself face-to-face with the king.
Eager to please, the *gracioso* answers Pedro's questions with
evasive responses. Pedro teases him, obviously enjoying his
antics and witticisms, but always maintaining the decorum
required of his position as king. He asks Galindo what he
is seeking in the palace. Galindo replies «Un escarpín a be-
sar,/ Porque los pies fuera (n) andar.» (I, xii). Pedro's
gently reproving reply shows his enjoyment of Galindo's
pun: «¡Grosero! Razón tenéis.»

The king asks him about the identity of his master, his
reason for his presence at court, and his own name. Galindo accommodatingly answers: «A quien quisiéreis, señor...
A lo que Vos/ Mandáreis... Como gustáreis.» Pedro observes ironically: «Estáis muy cortés.» Although Pedro
feels scorn for the fear of the *gracioso*: «Vuestros temores
condeno,» he admits that he is amused by him. Rather
than being severe with him for having entered his presence
unannounced, Pedro merely teases him. He does not judge
him by the same stringent standards which he would expect
of a man of the noble class, and he delights in seeing in
him the very trait which he despises in men of higher
station: his evasive cowardice.

---

of the incident. He views a scorn for the *gracioso* as a manifestation
of his self-control and *entereza*, which precludes his approval of the
frivolity of court buffoonery. Watson believes that this bargain
reflects Calderón's disapproval of the *hombres de burlas* which
were so much a part of the court of Felipe IV, and which served to
distract the king from his duties. He cites examples from Golden
Age writers who consider buffoons a dangerous element in the
Spanish court, and he offers evidence that it may well have been
a practice in Calderón's day for buffoons to have their teeth drawn
for the amusement of the courtiers. He emphasizes the fact that
at no time does Calderón's Pedro indicate that he would enjoy
seeing Coquín's teeth pulled, and since he does not actually punish
him, the bargain may well have been intended to show Pedro's
clemency rather than his cruelty. The scenes between the king
and the *gracioso* in Calderón's play lack the light-hearted banter
of Lope's original play.

When Galindo asks the king what he may do to serve him, Pedro says that he desires his presence merely for diversion: «Nada, que gusto de veros.» Although the *gracioso's* dramatic purpose for entering at this moment is to announce the arrival of Jacinto and Enrique, Lope has taken advantage of this short scene to give the audience insight into Pedro's sense of humor and his affection for this representative of the common people.

Another amusing exchange between Galindo and Pedro takes place in Act II when Pedro orders the room cleared so that he may hear the complaint of Jacinto in private. Galindo jokingly asks if he, too, must leave. One can almost hear Pedro chuckle as he says: «El primero has de salir.» (II, ix). After Pedro has brought about the reconciliation of Jacinto and Alvaro, Galindo interrupts their conversation to say that he, too, is a man of action and valor, and that he aspires to an appointment in which he may kill without being seen. When Pedro asks him what this position may be, Galindo reveals that it is that of royal chronicler. [13] It is obvious that Pedro enjoys acting as «straight man» to the *gracioso's* jokes. Rather than detracting from his self-possession as king, this fact serves to show his very human sense of humor.

In *El médico de su honra* Lope has again presented the human side of King Pedro. As in *Ya anda la de Mazagatos* we see a man who sincerely loves the common man and enjoys candid conversation and light-hearted banter as a diversion from his heavy responsibilities. Although he

---

[13] This reference may well be a reflection of Lope's own desire to secure the post. See H. N. Bershas, «Lope de Vega and the Post of Royal Chronicler,» *Hispanic Review*, XXI (April, 1963), 109-117. Another autobiographical reference on the part of Galindo may be found in Act II when he laments the tiresome duty as Jacinto's servant and wonders if service in the king's armada might not be a better use of his talents. Lope went along on the fateful voyage of 1588.

is a conscientious king who is vigilant in matters of honor and who is seriously concerned about the true opinions of his people concerning himself and his actions, he has a great weakness: his blind trust in his brother Enrique.

By failing to allow for the possibility of Enrique's guilt, Pedro creates a situation in which he can no longer maintain his impartiality as king. His complacency shattered, his reaction is all too human. Although he remains outwardly confident of his position as king, the treachery of the Infante and his own reaction to it undermine his inner sense of security, and he compensates by resolving to make a greater effort to be worthy of his high position. The conflict between the brothers, which was only suggested in *La niña de plata*, is now an established fact.

In both *El médico de su honra* and *La niña de plata* Pedro exhibits his personal valor and his spirit of adventure by going out in disguise to «rondar la calle.» Whereas in *La niña de plata* he was mainly interested in enacting a plan which he had devised to aid his brother, in *El médico de su honra* he is also attempting to fulfil his role as *rey justiciero* by hearing first-hand opinions of his people concerning his management of the affairs of the realm.

Although in neither play does he show a dread of omens or prognostications of future events, in *La niña de plata* and *El médico de su honra* Pedro does begin to lose some of his self-confidence. He suffers a disappointment in his relationship with his brother which causes him to act imprudently, reacting more as a man than as a king, a fact which results in a loss of some of his inner security, which manifests itself in a growing suspicion of everyone around him.

CHAPTER V

THE PASSIONS OVERTAKE THE MAN

In both *Lo cierto por lo dudoso* and *La carbonera* we see Pedro as a *galán enamorado* who is frustrated in his attempts to win the object of his desire. In *Lo cierto por lo dudoso* his rival is his own brother Enrique and there is suspicion and mounting tension between the brothers throughout the play. This mistrust of Enrique breeds a growing sense of insecurity in Pedro which is even more obvious in *La carbonera,* in which Pedro is so fearful of his brother's ambition that he seeks to kill his half-sister so that she will be unable to help him.

As Pedro's insecurity increases he is guilty of more frequent incidents of rash and emotional behavior such as we saw in his final scene with Enrique in *El médico de su honra.* His emotions and his personal desires play a larger role in his decisions, and he begins to show very real doubts that he will be able to maintain his position as king. His delight in hunting and his desire for contact with the common people begin to take on more the aspect of a purely emotional desire to escape from his problems rather than a temporary distraction. He is extremely serious in his outlook and there are no more demonstrations of his sense of humor such as we observed in *El médico de su honra*.

The friction between the brothers Pedro and Enrique is evident throughout the play *Lo cierto por lo dudoso*. On the other hand, another brother, the Maestre de Santiago,[1] is the constant companion of the king. Although for the purposes of the play itself the friction between Pedro and Enrique is no more than the superficial tension which naturally arises between two rivals for the attentions of a lady, when we compare their relationship in this play with that evident in *La niña de plata* or *El médico de su honra* we detect none of the brotherly affection which Pedro displayed toward the unhappy Enrique in *La niña de plata* nor the trust which led him to confide his thoughts to him in *El médico de su honra*. Their mutual suspicion is evident in the early scenes of the play. Since these scenes also reveal important aspects of Pedro's characterization as a *galán enamorado*, we shall examine them in some detail.

In the very first scene of *La niña de plata* Enrique and his companion Ramiro are enjoying the festivities of the «noche de San Juan» when the king and the Maestre approach them. Enrique tries to avoid his brother, but Pedro sees him before he can escape: «Enrique, ¡tanto cuidado!/ ¿De mí te guardas?» (I, ii). Enrique counters this accusation with another, referring to the king's disguise: «Señor/ Antes pensé que tu eras/ El que guardarte quisieras.» Enrique's irritation is evident in his reply to Pedro's question about his activities: «Ya ¿no lo ve Vuestra Alteza?» When Pedro chides him for his apparently aimless wanderings, Enrique's irritation breaks into open hostility: «¡Por Dios, señor, que he salido/ Sólo a escuchar disparates/ Esta noche!»

_____
[1] Lope calls this brother Tello, although in history he was Fadrique.

Mendo tries to cover for his rude outburst, but Pedro
does not appear to be upset or offended by it. He asks his
brother what he has observed on his *ronda*. Enrique replies that he has been listening to music and observing the
people, and he adds that he has also engaged no fewer than
four men in a test of skill at swordsmanship. Pedro expresses an approval of this activity which recalls the king
of *La niña de plata* when he says of Enrique: «No hay en
España/ Tal brío.» Pedro asks Enrique to take him along
with him on his wanderings. Enrique replies that such
frivolous activities as those characteristic of this celebration
could not be of much interest to a king.

After the men discuss some of the customs of the day [2]
and express their opinions concerning the duplicity of certain women, it is Pedro who injects a positive note into the
conversation by observing that such considerations as a
woman's appearance are, after all, superficial, and that
women, for all their faults, are still man's greatest delight:

> ¡Por Dios, que donde no están
> Que no hay gusto ni alegría,
> Ni del hombre compañía
> Como la que ellas le dan!
> Lindas enfermeras son
> De alma y cuerpo. (I, i).

This short speech reveals a sentimentality which we have
not observed heretofore in Lope's plays which treat king

---

[2] Mendo observes that all of the unmarried girls would be
occupied with their ritual of prayers for a future husband. According to this custom, the first name of an eligible man that a girl
hears after her prayer is that of her future spouse. Ramiro mentions the Spanish custom of placing a glass of water on the
windowsill into which to break an egg at the stroke of midnight
in order to see in the shape assumed by the liquid the likeness of a
future bridegroom. For a discussion of these and other customs,
see John T. Reid, «St. John's Day in Spanish Literature», *Hispania*, XVIII (1935), 401-412.

Pedro. In his role as a *galán enamorado*, Pedro will express frequent opinions about love and the opposite sex.

When Enrique complains of the fickleness of women
Pedro sees his chance to question his brother concerning
which ladies have aroused his interest. It becomes obvious
that Enrique is trying to conceal his love for a lady for
whom Pedro also feels an attraction, for when Enrique
says that there are two ladies whom he fancies, one attain-
able, and the other impossible for him, Pedro begins to press
him to reveal the name of the unattainable lady, revealing
in an aside the extent of his own passion and jealousy:
«Más me mata, más me abrasa.»

The men stop at the door of Teodora, and Enrique begs
her to keep his brother occupied while he leaves to attend
to another matter. When Pedro notices that he is missing
and asks where he is, he is obviously irritated that his brother has succeeded in eluding him. Angry and suspicious of
his brother, he tells the Maestre that he is ready to leave
Teodora's house: «¡Que pueda Enrique tener/ Licencia para
engañarme!» (I, iv). Teodora observes the king's jealousy:
«Que la mayor majestad/ Pone el amor a sus pies.»

Pedro has thus shown in his first appearance in the
play the fact that as a man he suffers from jealousy and
can fall in love the same as any other man in the kingdom.

Pedro's hesitation to reveal to the father of the lady
Juana his desire to marry her is the source of most of the
plot complications in the play. Aside from being essential
to the dramatic action, this hesitation also reveals a very
real sense of insecurity on the part of Pedro which springs
from his growing distrust of Enrique. It is this lack of
self-confidence and the fear of Enrique's success in his
courtship of Juana which cause Pedro to engage in a elabo-
rate deception which will lead to the frustration of his own
desires.

In Act II Pedro speaks with Juana's father, who is his

adelantado mayor, and he tells him that he wants to reward his loyal service by arranging for the marriage of his daughter with a man who is his own equal. Had he revealed the fact that the intended bridegroom was he himself, he might have been successful in winning the hand of Juana. As the *adelantado* and his men depart after the interview, Pedro again reveals his admiration for bravery and manly prowess as he observes that the victories of his soldiers add to the force of his own love.

When the Maestre says rather cynically that he thinks Pedro is seeking to fulfil his own desires at the expense of the honor of his loyal *adelantado,* Pedro tells him without hesitation that he intends to make Juana his queen. When he tells the Maestre not to court Juana's cousin Inés out of courtesy to him, Pedro reveals the extent of his own love for Juana:

> Que amor no es bien que se trate
> Menos que como es el mío,
> Que ruego, peno y porfío,
> Y gusto de que me mate. (II, III).

A conversation between the *adelantado,* his daughter, and his niece Inés concerning the enigmatic proposal of the king that he marry Juana to an unnamed gentleman of the very highest social rank serves to emphasize the seriousness of Pedro's error in not telling the father the whole truth. The *adelantado's* natural conclusion is that Pedro intends to marry her to one of his brothers. When Inés suggests that Pedro may be intending to marry her himself, the father refuses to place his hopes in such a match without a clearer statement of intention on the part of the king in order to spare himself the possible disappointment. In a later interview when Pedro tells the father of his arrangements for the betrothal ceremony he is still reluctant to admit that it is he who is the intended bridegroom.

He merely says that the *adelantado* will soon be a relative of his. The father says that either of the two brothers of the king would please him as a husband for his daughter. Pedro lets pass this excellent opportunity to state his own love and increase the honor of his gesture to his loyal subject. He tells Mendo to summon the Archbishop and tells the father that it is his wish that he secretly marry Juana to «un hombre/ Tan bueno como yo.« (III, X).

When the father asks the name of the man Pedro evades the question by saying: «Basta que le veáis.» The *adelantado* is now certain that his future son-in-law is one of the king's brothers. He expresses his preference for Enrique, but when he hears that he is in exile he concludes that the man can be none other than the Maestre.

It is difficult to understand the hesitation of Pedro to tell the father of his own love for Juana. Pedro has little reason to doubt his own attractiveness as a suitor. He might indeed have won the lady's hand on his merits in spite of her love for Enrique, for she admits that she finds Pedro extremely attractive:

> El Rey, cuando no tuviera
> Más de ser rey, ¿a qué amor
> No deshiciera el rigor?
> ¿Qué peña no enterneciera?
> Cuanto y más, siendo galán,
> Entendido, fuerte, hermoso,
> A pie y a caballo airoso;
> Que la noche de San Juan
> Que le vi, me pareció
> Que era ingratitud no amalle. (II, viii).

Pedro's own personal interest in the lady Juana causes him to treat his brother Enrique unjustly on several occasions in the play. Pedro's first interview with Juana ends in a confrontation between the brothers which brings about Pedro's abrupt and unjust banishment of Enrique. The

king arrives at Juana's house on the flimsy excuse of wanting to see the beautifully decorated altar she has prepared.
When Juana mentions the fact that this visit endangers her
honor, since her father is away, Pedro immediately expresses his purely honorable intentions.

Pedro asks Juana if she has said her prayer for a husband, hoping that he has been the first to appear after the
event and that he will thus be able to win her favor. Juana
avoids the subject, claiming not to believe in the custom.
Pedro tries to discover if Enrique has arrived ahead of him,
but Juana denies that she has seen him. At this moment
the alarm on Enrique's watch sounds, [3] and he is forced to
reveal himself.

Pedro is so angered at seeing his brother that he
impulsively and unceremoniously banishes him from the
court: «Sal, Enrique, desta corte,/ No estés el San Juan en
ella,/ Pues me das tan mal San Juan.» (I, xi). His reason for
banishing his brother is a purely selfish one. He has allowed
his personal feelings of jealousy to cause him to act
unjustly. Pedro refuses to listen even to his brother the
Maestre who tries to reason with him, and he places an
unreasonable condition on his offer of pardon for Enrique:
that he may remain only if he renounces his courtship of
Juana. Enrique tries to pretend that it was Inés whom
he had been courting, but Pedro is not deceived. He tells
Ramiro to be certain that Enrique leaves the city.

Before he leaves her house, Pedro expresses his love to
Juana and tells her that he wants her to become his queen.
The Maestre advises Juana to forget Enrique and to receive
the king's suit: «Que no es de mujer prudente/ No levantar
a la frente/ Corona que os pone al pie.» (I, xiv).

A second confrontation between the brothers occurs

---

[3] The introduction of this device into this play which treats
a fourteenth-century king is an obvious anachronism.

when Enrique returns secretly from his exile. Although he feels certain that he has lost Juana's love and that she will accept the suit of the king, he cannot resist seeing her once more, and he goes to her house as soon as it is dark. Pedro has also come in disguise to speak of his love to Juana. The Maestre, who is instructed by Pedro to detain Enrique and wait for his return, decides instead to seek the king as soon as he sees Enrique approaching for fear that he might flee before Pedro could talk with him.

The words of Ramiro, who is apprehensive at the thought of meeting the king in disguise, serve to emphasize the advantage which Pedro has over his brother and all other men of the kingdom by virtue of his position as king, and they serve also to underline the injustice of his arbitrary exile of Enrique for purely personal reasons: «¿Tengo yo de medir a un Rey la espada,/ Que llega, cuando quiere sin medida,/ De un reino a otro, y sólo Dios le juzga?» (II, xxi). Pedro reveals his failure to win the affections of Juana as he enters the stage after their interview at her window: «No hay orden que a quererme la reduzga.» (II, xxii). Enrique hides his face and hears Pedro's words, which the king believes to be directing to the Maestre:

>   Maestre, ¿ha venido Enrique?
>   Que ya prevenida queda
>   Doña Inés, y ¡vive Dios
>   Que hoy se ha de casar por fuerza! (II, xxii).

Pedro adds that Juana had become angry at his coming to visit her uninvited and unannounced, and that she had been weeping because of Enrique's absence.

When the silent figure does not respond, Pedro approaches him and discovers that his hearer is Enrique himself, who expresses his dismay that he has caused the king so much displeasure that he would force him to marry against his will a woman whom does not love. Enrique tells his brother that Inés has undoubtedly tricked Pedro into believing that he was in love with her. [*]

Pedro asks Enrique how he has dared to violate the terms of his exile when he had given his word to abide by them. Enrique answers that he never gave his word not to love Juana. He states that he has come out only after dark so that no one may know of his return to the city and so that he may in this manner maintain the outward appearance of observing the terms of his banishment.

Pedro reminds Enrique that he can have him taken into custody for violation of the law, and he demands that he turn his sword over to him. Enrique hands it to him without resistance. When Pedro calls him a traitor Enrique appeals to him as a brother for clemency: «Soy tu hermano./ Nunca mi madre fue reina;/ Pero fue tu padre el mío.» (II, xxii). Pedro replies sternly: «Enrique, no me enternezcas.» Enrique refuses to remain, saying that he is ashamed at having his brother see his weakness. Pedro makes no move to detain Enrique or to call for help. He is so amazed at the firmness of Enrique's resolution that he hesitates too long and allows him to escape.

In this scene Lope contrasts the positive actions of Enrique with the uncertainty of Pedro, who is renderd inactive by the realization that he has not acted fairly toward his brother. Enrique is presented more sympathetically as the innocent victim of a personal whim on the part of his brother. He is respectful toward Pedro in spite of the injustice which he has shown him, and he emerges from this scene as an admirable character who has demonstrated the strength of his convictions without openly defying the authority of the king.

When the Maestre and Mendo reenter and find Pedro

---

[*] Inés had in fact intercepted a letter from Enrique to Juana and had deceitfully showed it to Pedro as proof of Enrique's supposed love for her.

alone with the Infante's sword still in his hands, the king reveals his frustration and his realization that he himself has created this unusual situation by his own selfishness: «¡Maldiga el cielo estas puertas,/ O maldiga mi desdicha!/ Que no está la culpa en ellas.» (II, xxiii).

Enrique is aware of the seriousness of his position and yet he persists in his courtship of Juana. He reproaches her for her interest in becoming queen which has made her forget her former love for him, and he reminds her of the extent of his sacrifice for love of her: «Soy el que perdió por ti/ Su Rey, su hermano, su dueño.» (III, iii). He reveals his helplessness to prevent the king from marrying Juana:

> Nací de rey; mas ¿qué importa?
> No hay fuerza contra la suya.
> Rey poderoso, y mi hermano,
> ¡Qué de respetos se juntan! (III, iii).

In contrast to his severity and lack of compassion for his brother Enrique, the attitude of Pedro toward Juana is one of tender affection. He demonstrates his eagerness to please her in his discussion of their choice of residence:

> Y si no quieres tú que aquí resida,
> Luego verás a Guadarrama helado;
> Que como tengo en ti mi propia vida
> Y el reino de mi amor depositado,
> Adonde tú quisieres, allí sea
> La corte, donde yo te goce y vea. (III, vi).

Pedro devises a clever test to determine the degree of Juana's attraction to Enrique. He pretends to have received a letter from his brother in Córdoba asking for his pardon and requesting that he arrange a marriage for him in Sevilla. Pedro asks Juana if she can suggest a lady who might be a suitable wife for the Infante. She takes this opportunity to confess that she believes that it is she whom the

Infante loves, and that, although she is honored by the king's attentions, she would prefer to marry Enrique.

Pedro and Inés conspire together to arrange for a double betrothal ceremony for that same evening at which Pedro will marry Juana and Inés will marry Enrique. It is obvious that Pedro has not suffered any serious disillusionment from Juana's expression of preference for Enrique, for he tells Inés to inform Juana that he has no intention of marrying her to Enrique, and that he is interpreting her disclosure as evidence of her desire to inspire jealousy in him as a proof of his devotion.

Alone on stage, Pedro speaks in a lovely sonnet of the frustrations of the gentle emotion of love. The tender sentiments and the imaginative comparisons of this poem reveal a sensitivity which is appropriate to his role as a *galán enamorado*:

> ¡Con qué justa razón a la esperanza
> Dieron nombre de flor, pues que la imita
> En que tan brevemente se marchita,
> Que tiene entre las hojas la mudanza!
> Lustrosas perlas a la aurora alcanza,
> De matizados círculos escrita;
> Belleza que la noche solicita
> Para perder su ardor en su templanza.
> Sembraba yo, porque la tierra nueva
> Me prometió de amor ricos favores:
> ¡Ay, loco engaño, de mis celos prueba!
> ¿De qué sirve sembrar locos amores,
> Si viene un desengaño que se lleva
> Arboles, ramas, hojas, fruto y flores? (II, xvi).

Pedro sends the Maestre to Juana with the crown of Castilla on a covered tray with the message: «A vuestros pies,/ Cuanto y más a vuestra frente, / La ofrece el Rey.» (III, xiv). Juana is surprised at the gesture, and she does not know how to respond to it. Confused, she asks that Pedro come to see her. Alone with her companion Elvira,

Juana addresses the crown as if it were a person, giving the reasons for her resolution not to accept it:

> Diga el interés celoso
> Que hay mujer que supo amar,
> Perder un reino, y dejar
> Lo cierto por lo dudoso. (III, xv).

Since the crown is the symbol of Pedro's position as king, this is her official answer to his suit. However, since Pedro as a man has lost his objectivity in his desire to marry her in spite of her resistance, the rational answer must be addressed to the external symbol rather than to the person of the king. The acceptance of her decision by Pedro as a man must await the frustration of his scheme to have his own way in spite of her wishes.

When he comes to see Juana as bidden, Pedro senses her confusión, and he reveals once again his own insecurity:

> El Maestre me avisó
> Que me querías hablar;
> Y el alma en otro lugar
> Confusas nuevas me dio;
> Porque también me previno
> Mi hermano de que turbada
> Le respondistes. (III, xvi).

Juana tells him that her news may upset him. Pedro states that he wants to know the truth even though it may not please him. When Juana finally admits her love for Enrique, Pedro makes a calm and calculated decision to kill his brother if it is necessary in order to have Juana for his queen. He is fully aware of the treachery of his resolution.

He realizes that he is acting in response to his passions, which have temporarily blinded his powers of reason:

Pero yo, que ya ofendido
Y celoso estoy de modo,
Que los ojos cierro a todo,
Enamorado y corrido,
Ni a los necios he temido
Ni a los discretos tampoco;
Antes más bien me provoco
A satisfacer mi injuria;
Que no hay venganza sin furia
Ni amor sin punta de loco. (III, xvi).

In spite of this awareness that he is acting selfishly and unjustly, Pedro coolly and calmly states his reasons for wanting his brother killed:

Muera Enrique, porque muerto
Me casaré con viuda,
Si el amor pusiere duda
En la verdad del concierto:
Con esto, aunque descubierto
Quede lo que has referido,
Tu y yo no habremos perdido
Honor, pues en tal suceso
Serás viuda de un beso,
Como otras de su marido. (III, vi).

Juana is greatly upset by the king's decision, and she plans to write to Enrique telling him to flee to France, England or even Granada in order to escape Pedro's vengeance. This detail is reminiscent of the prophecy of the Moor Zulema in La niña de plata who told the disbelieving Enrique that he would be forced to flee Castilla for fear of his brother's wrath.

Elvira informs Juana that Enrique has come in disguise to witness the betrothal ceremony in an effort to forget her more easily by actually seeing her give her consent to marry his brother Pedro. Juana's father tells her of the arrival of the Archbishop and he remarks upon the sullen aspect of the king and the tears of the intended bride. He is confused by the undertone of uncertainty which pervades the entire group which has assembled to witness the ceremony: «Todos hablan de secreto,/ Y a todos estoy mirando.» (III, xx). Inés, intending to avenge herself for Enrique's scorn, tells the *adelantado* of the Infante's secret presence in Elvira's room. Believing him to be the intended bridegroom, the father goes to welcome him.

Meanwhile, Pedro tells the Maestre that he has sent his men all over the kingdom to seek out and kill Enrique. The Maestre pleads with Pedro not to carry out his cruel intention.

The Maestre knows that the betrothal ceremony between Enrique and Juana has already taken place, and he reproaches Pedro for keeping such an important matter a secret from the people, who have the right to know of the projected marriage of any member of the royal family. Pedro is still unaware of the result that his complicated plan has had, but he notices the consternation of all those present in the house of the *adelantado*. Pedro admits that he has been in error in keeping the royal betrothal a secret: «Confieso que yerro, y hago/ Una cosa sin razón,/ Que no la entiendo y la trato.» (III, xxiii).

This admission and the earlier threats against the life of Enrique contribute to the suspense of the audience concerning Pedro's reaction to the fact of his loss of Juana to his brother. When he learns the truth, Pedro admits that this turn of events was the direct result of his own error in keeping his intention to marry Juana such a closely-guarded secret. He is frustrated, but resigned, and he not only recognizes the betrothal but he also pardons Enrique for his violation of the exile which he had imposed upon him. He tells Juana to have the crown which she has refused painted backwards on her coat-of-arms. This is an ironic touch, since she will later become queen through the death of Pedro himself.

In *Lo cierto por lo dudoso* King Pedro is not so self-confident as was the king of the *Audiencias, Ya anda la de Mazagatos, La niña de plata* or *El médico de su honra*. He has less control over his own passions and he makes judgments which stem from his emotional mood of the moment rather than from a careful examination of the facts of a situation with proper attention to possible effects of his decisions. Far from being a devoted and trusting brother, he is suspicious and self-centered to such a degree that he coldly plans the murder of Enrique in order to prevent him from interfering with his personal desires.

On the other hand, as a *galán enamorado* he is considerate, sensitive, and eager to please the lady who is the object of his affections. The curious dichotomy of virtues and vices in his ambivalent nature includes the extremes of vengefulness and violent passions and sensitivity. The overall impression is that of an unstable individual who, as a judge, may be unduly severe at one moment and lenient to the point of permissiveness the next.

The Pedro of *La carbonera* is also a man of extremes. Although he is concerned about his reputation as a wise and just king, he allows his desire for diversion from his duties to remove him from the center of political activity for long periods of time and he ruthlessly pursues an innocent half-sister because of his almost paranoic fear of his brother Enrique, whom he suspects may use her marital eligibility to further his own interests in the Castilian civil war.

As a *galán enamorado* Pedro is as considerate and compassionate as the king of *Lo cierto por lo dudoso* until his desires are frustrated. His situation in *La carbonera* is highly ironical, since the object of his vengeance and the object of his affection are one and the same and he will be frustrated in both of the undertakings which preoccupy his mind: his love for the disguised Leonor and his desire to wreak vengeance upon his rival Enrique by means of the murder of his half-sister.

King Pedro is the first dramatic character to enter the stage, and his speech sets the tone for the entire play. He states that whereas he is usually gladdened by his arrival in Sevilla, this visit is a source of pain for him since his reason for coming is to seek out an enemy who poses a threat to his position as king. He reveals his insecurity, suspicion, and his desire for vengeance, setting a mood of sinister anticipation which suggests the possibility of violence during the course of the dramatic action:

> ¡Como si no bastaran sus hermanos,
> Que de mi honor pretenden ser tiranos!
> Pero yo los pondré presto de suerte,
> Que asegure mi vida con su muerte. (I, i).

The nobleman Juan Velasco expresses his amazement at the king's immediately aggressive attitude toward this sister, the existence of whom he had been unaware a scant ten days earlier: «¿Qué temes de ella? ¿Qué sospechas tienes,/ Que con tanto cuidado a verla vienes?» The sinister mood of this scene is reinforced by repeated references to Leonor de Guzmán, who is supposedly still alive and a prisoner of Pedro. Pedro refers to her as a kind of Hydra who seems to produce new offspring to threaten him even as he manages to contain those who are presently plaguing him:

> Donde una corta, otra cabeza crece;
> Comienza Enrique, y el Maestre cesa.
> ¿No le bastaba a esta mujer tirana
> Darme estos dos hermanos? (I, i).

Pedro tells Juan that his reason for seeking out his half-sister is fear of losing his crown: «Porque si ésta se casa ocultamente/ Con algún desleal a mi persona,/ ¿Cómo estará segura mi corona?» He orders Juan to find her and to take her into custody. His mounting insecurity is obvious:

> Que si hoy la prendo, morirá mañana.
> Esto me da cuidado, esto deseo;
> Quiero acabar con todos mis contrarios,
> Pues que ya a Enrique con las armas veo,
> Y buscando los modos necesarios
> Para quitarme el reino con la vida. (I, i).

Although he agrees that Enrique's pretensions are a danger to Pedro, the nobleman Fernando cannot understand why the king is so fearful of his half-sister. Pedro abruptly orders him to be silent and to obey him without further questions:

> No me replique el que mi gusto precisa;
> Yo sé lo que me importa y me conviene.
> Quien sangre alguna de esta casa tiene,
> No fíe, cuando piense en mi grandeza,
> Que tiene muy segura la cabeza. (I, i).

He admonishes his subjects to obey without complaint or offer of advice, and shows his need to reassure himself that he commands the respect of his followers: «Que aunque ha de ser la Majestad amada,/ Nunca más respetada/ Que cuando fue temida.»

As Leonor enters the stage for first time she reinforces the mood of foreboding that was so evident in the first scene by mentioning the imprisonment of her mother. She complains of Pedro's cruelty and states that she is certain that her own death will follow soon after that of her mother. Her servant Tello agrees that her only hope is escape, since she cannot possibly expect mercy from the «arrogancia e ira» of Pedro. He suggests that she try to write to her brother Enrique for help, observing that she is justified in her fear of Pedro: «Que es de condición terrible.»

Juan comes to take Leonor to the king, but he hesitates to do so, for he immediately falls in love with her and is fearful for her safety:

> Temo que os mate, Leonor,
> Porque en condición tan dura,
> No halla puerta la hermosura,
> Ni tiene entrada el amor. (I, vi).

He allows her to escape. She takes refuge with the family of a *carbonero* with whom she had lived for six years in seclusion from the jealous Queen María de Portugal. Laurencio, the *carbonero*, comments upon the severity of King Pedro and mentions a prophecy very similar to the one of Zulema in *La niña de plata*:

> Conozco bien las crueldades
> Del Rey y lo que aborrece
> Los generosos Guzmanes,
> Que hay pronóstico en Castilla,
> Que dice que han de heredarle;
> Que es bien que en hombres crueles
> Las sucesiones se acaben. (I, x).

Leonor and her companion Inés disguise themselves as Laurencio's nieces. Leonor laments the cruel intention of the king: «¡Ay, Pedro, tu hermana soy!/ ¡No quiera Dios que me mates!»

Pedro is angry that Leonor has escaped his vengeance. Juan tells him rather cryptically that love had protected the beautiful Leonor and had prevented him from taking her into custody. Pedro naturally supposes that it was Enrique's help which made her escape possible, and he suspects that there must be a spy in his court who had aided in the escape. Pedro is so insecure and fearful of losing his crown that he suspects almost everyone around him.

In order to forget for a while his problems with Enrique and Leonor, Pedro orders preparations for the hunt. This scene in which he comes into contact with the common people after becoming separated from his hunting party is very similar to the meeting of the king and the villagers of Mazagatos. Once in the open country, Pedro works off his frustrations by tiring himself physically. He seeks shade from the hot sun, and he asks the peasant Bras where he may find shelter in order to rest from his exercise. Bras is interested in learning the identity of this nobleman. He asks Pedro if he is one of the courtiers of the king or if he is of the rival Guzmán family: «Que persigue el rey don Pedro / Con temor del conde Enrique.» (I, xiv).

Pedro shows clearly in his answer that he does not wish to discuss his official problems on this outing, and he pretends to be a member of the minor nobility who knows nothing of political affairs:

> La paz y quietud pretendo
> Que busca un buen ciudadano;
> Bien se ve, amigo, pues vengo
> Cazando por estos montes,
> Entretenimiento honesto. (I, xiv).

When he inquires if there is a house nearby in which he may rest, Bras praises the comfort and hospitality of Laurencio's home, saying that, although it is humble, its owner is as satisfied with it as is the king with his splendid palace, which is full of many problems which the *carbonero* does not share. Pedro agrees that the king does have many problems!

Bras offers his candid opinion of the king: «Dalde a los diablos, que pienso/ Que ha de pasar a cochillo/ Todo lo mejor del reino.» Pedro calmly defends his reputation: «Eso tiene el vulgo loco:/ Que siendo un rey justiciero,/ Luego dice que es cruel.» This is the first indication so far in the play of a defense of Pedro against his imputed cruelty. Bras does not deny the good qualities of the king, but he criticizes his pride and his impulsive tendency to take swift and severe vengeance for any offense: «¡Mal año, que por el suelo/ Ruedan setenta cabezas!»

Pedro calmly asks if this vengeance is not justified when it is taken upon those who are guilty of crimes against the Crown. Bras disagrees with the indiscriminate severity implicit in this statement. He suggests that the king is an unduly severe judge without the redeeming quality of mercy: «Es tan fiero,/ Que, cual segador, derriba/ Altos y bajos al suelo.» Pedro refers to his father's reputation as a valiant warrior against the Moors and he asks Bras if King Pedro is any less worthy than King Alfonso had been. Bras replies simply that although the king is brave he is also cruel.

Bras supposes the king to be in Toledo. He mentions the death of Leonor de Guzmán in Talavera, and he attributes the deed to Pedro. As he is telling of the escape of Leonor the two men arrive at Laurencio's home.

Throughout this conversation Pedro has remained almost impassively calm while hearing the most serious charges of cruelty against himself. He has been able to separate his emotions from his office and to see himself in his role as king through the eyes of another person. He has allowed Bras to do most of the talking and he has not tried to defend his image too vehemently. He seems more interested in learning the true opinions of Bras than in making an effort to change what he considers to be a mistaken impression of himself.

Pedro's attitude in this scene has actually belied most of what Bras has said about his supposed impulsive nature and his thirst for vengeance against anyone who offends him. Had we not witnessed his zeal for vengeance in the first scene of the play it would indeed be difficult to believe such an attitude of the calm and self-contained king of this scene.

Pedro compliments Laurencio on his house and asks him about his family. Laurencio has chairs brought so that the men may be comfortable as they converse. He observes with rather biting satirical remarks the custom at court of denying chairs to those for whom one wishes to show scorn or displeasure. He also criticizes the rampant slander of the court. Pedro hears all of this criticism calmly and does not take issue with the *carbonero*. He seems genuinely interested in finding out more about Laurencio and his way of life.

Laurencio expresses his gratitude that it has not been necessary for him to borrow money from the usurers in the city who charge high interest rates. Pedro starts to say that if the king were aware of this evil practice he might take steps to correct it, but Laurencio interrupts him: «Ya yo sé que es justo y grave;/ Pero si el Rey no lo sabe,/ ¿Qué importa?» (I, xv). Pedro asures him that the king is always interested in learning of such abuses and that he is ever the defender of the oppressed.

Pedro asks to meet the other members of the family. He takes an interest in each one, asking what their duties are. He is especially attracted to Laura, who is in reality his disguised half-sister Leonor. He tells her that she is far lovelier than the ladies of Sevilla. At this moment Juan Velasco and the other courtiers enter and the king's disguise is ended. All of the peasant characters are dismayed to learn that their candid observations have been directed to none other than the King Pedro of whom all fear swift vengeance for the slightest cause. Bras is particularly fearful: «Hoy nos manda matar.» (I, xvii).

Pedro tells Juan Velasco to find out more about the lovely Laura. Although he laments in an aside the fact that Leonor has happened to meet the king under these

circumstances, Juan remains outwardly calm and he assures
the king that he will bring her to him to entertain him
during his rest.

In Act II, after Pedro has returned to Sevilla, Leonor and
Inés discuss the irony of the situation, and Leonor states
that she knows that it would be impossible for Pedro to
allow her to live if he learned her identity in spite of the
fact that he is so fond of her. Leonor believes that Pedro's
love for her is a punishment for his cruelty. Leonor gives
Bras a letter to be taken to Juan in Sevilla which supposedly
concerns arrangements for an organ [5] for the town church
which Pedro has ordered.

Meanwhile Pedro has learned that his half-sister is not
with Enrique as he had believed. He is saddened by the
realization that she has successfully escaped him, and
dramatic irony is prominent in his statement to Juan that
his greatest consolation from his problems is the company
of the lovely peasant girl Laura.

With the words: «Que me cansan cuidados del Palacio.»
(II, v). Pedro orders preparations for a hunting trip which
is to last eight or ten days. This action of King Pedro is
consistent with his natural preference for the simple pleasures of the hunt and his natural desire for a respite from
his responsibilities. However, the timing and the length
of the retreat are the result of a poorly calculated decision
in view of his pressing need to locate his half-sister now
that he is certain that she has not found permanent refuge
with her brother Enrique. His lack of perseverance in the
search reveals a serious lack of prudence in Pedro both
as king and as a man of common sense.

The practical realities of his situation demand that Pedro
remove this threat to the security of his official position
by capturing the lady. He should be making every effort

---

[5]   This is another obvious anachronism in a play dealing with a
fourteenth-century king.

to ensure the capture of the elusive half-sister whose marital eligibility would be such a powerful weapon in the hands of the ambitious Enrique. This is indeed a most unfortunate time for him be seeking escape from his duties, and the very fact that he is willing and able to forget such pressing official matters in a time of crisis for his reign suggests that he is not fulfilling his responsibility as king. He has allowed his personal inclinations to interfere with his duties as king to the point where he has needlessly endangered his own position.

This King Pedro is far from the conscientious monarch of *El médico de su honra* who bent every effort to be available at all times to his subjects even to the point of leaving the side of his unconscious brother in order to return to his duties at court. Also, the hunting excursion of Pedro in *Ya anda la de Mazagatos* which necessitated a delay in his hearing of the complaint of Alvaro and Juan was only a brief interlude compared with this protracted diversion. It is clear that the King Pedro of this play is much less a king and more a man than the Pedro of either the *Audiencias, Ya anda la de Mazagatos,* or *El médico de su honra.*

When Bras arrives at the palace to deliver the letter from Leonor to Juan he comes face-to-face with the king. In his confusion he says to Pedro: «Deme su merced el pie/ Que se hallare más a mano». (II, vii). Contrary to his procedure in *El médico de su honra* in Pedro's scene with Galindo, Lope does not take advantage of this opportunity to allow King Pedro to demonstrate a sense of humor. Either he does not detect, or he chooses to ignore the humor of the unintentional pun of Bras, and he merely asks him who he is and what his mission is at the court.

When Bras mentions the *órganos* Pedro supposes that this must be a name for some rich cloth or veiling which Laura wants as a gift. There is humor in this scene, but it is unintentional, and the stern and somber countenance of the king may remain unchanged throughout. Pedro asks Bras what he would like for himself, and he asks for a pair of breeches so that he may appear more attractively attired for courtship. Pedro asks the name of the girl in whom Bras has such an interest. He compliments Bras on his good taste when he hears that it is Laura.

Throughout this scene Pedro has had ample opportunity to demonstrate a sense of humor. The king of *El médico de su honra* would certainly have teased Bras for his inadvertent pun and for his preoccupation with a new pair of breeches for purposes of courtship. This more serious Pedro merely says: «¿Los zaragüelles son galas?». At the end of this scene it is Pedro's very seriousness which occasions laughter when he tells Juan Velasco to find out what kind of cloth is known by the name of *órganos* so that he may take some to Laura.

When Pedro sees the disguised Leonor once again he tells her of his love and he promises to grant her whatever she wishes. She craftily elicits from him a solemn oath never to harm her. Pedro directs Juan to arrange for him to visit the *carbonero's* house in disguise that evening. When the two men arrive, Bras is already there. Pedro reveals a lack of circumspection when he says: «No le echaremos del puesto?». (II, xxii). Juan explains that this would cause a disturbance which might reveal the king's disguise and cause Laurencio to keep so close a watch on Laura that another interview might be impossible.

Pedro complains petulantly of his frustration: «Pues ¿éstos me han de quitar/ Mi gusto?». In this speech he reveals his total preoccupation with his own pleasures and shows little consideration for the embarassment or scandal that a nocturnal disturbance at Laurencio's house might cause the *carbonero*. The two men are forced to leave when the peasant Menga comes to spy on Bras, and Laurencio becomes aware of the activity outside of Laura's window.

In the opening scene of Act III [6] Leonor reveals her fear of telling Pedro the truth: «Es notable su crueldad;/ Pues ¿cómo será si entiende/ Que le engaño?» Pedro has returned to Sevilla and has sent for her to join him. Bras returns from the city and tells of having seen Pedro in the procession of the celebration of Corpus Christi. He describes with awe the appearance of the king:

> La majestad en los ojos,
> La grandeza en la persona,
> Diciendo que a sólo Dios
> Puede ser que reconozca. (III, ii).

This description of the semi-divine aspect of the royal majesty is totally different from the very human dramatic character of King Pedro who appears in this play.

Whereas the public person of King Pedro who appears in the procession inspires admiration and is aloof from his subjects, as a man Pedro has engaged in familiar conversation with both peasants and noblemen and has not retained in these scenes the aura of semi-divinity which is so evident in the description of Bras. By contrast Lope clearly intends that we understand that Pedro is appearing more as a man than as a king in this play.

Juan comes to take Leonor to the king, and he tells her of Pedro's willful disregard of anything which stands in the way of his determination to have her:

> A su alcázar me mandó
> Que te llevase, atrevido
> De amor; que ningún olvido

---

[6] The text of this act taken from the manuscript of the Biblioteca Nacional which is contained in Volume X of the new Academy edition of Lope's works does not differ significantly in the passages treating Pedro from the earlier edition.

> Contra su rigor bastó.
> Divertirle intenté yo;
> No le puede sosegar. (III, iii).

Laurencio suggests that Leonor pretend to be married and thus excuse herself from going to the palace. Juan approves of the *carbonero's* strategy as being consistent with the reaction which one might expect of Pedro as king and the guardian of his subjects' honor:

> Bien dices, porque él codicia
> Que a nadie fuerza se haga,
> Mayormente en el honor,
> Porque en esto, el más señor
> Cualquier agravio le paga. (III, iv).

Leonor tells Bras that he may become her husband as soon as he has given definite proof of his *limpieza de sangre*. This stalling technique will allow her to use the betrothal as a defense against Pedro's passion and at the same time shield her from the eager attentions of Bras himself.

Pedro tells Fernando that he has found Sevilla so charming that he plans to remain there for the rest of the summer. This fascination with the city and its association with the object of his passion is reminiscent of the historical Pedro's long residence in the Alcázar with his love María de Padilla. Pedro says that his love for Laura has wrought a marvelous change in him: «Con la propiedad que tiene,/ Mi condición ha templado.» (III, vi). These words are heavily laden with dramatic irony, for no sooner has he uttered them than Juan enters to tell him of Laura's supposed marriage, and the king demonstrates that his quick temper and vengefulness are unchanged.

Juan is confident of the king's resignation to forget Leonor once he learns that she is married. Juan feigns a willingness to bring her to him against her will:

Si casada la quieres,
Sacada de los brazos de un villano,
Como a mañana esperes,
Aunque gozada, la tendrá tu mano;
Que de ir contra las leyes,
A sólo Dios darán cuenta los reyes. (III, vii).

This timely reminder of the divine justice which awaits
the king who does not conform to the conduct expected of
God's earthly representative increases the seriousness of
Pedro's unexpected outburst of anger. He upbraids Juan
for not fighting all of the men of the town, if necessary,
in order to bring him the object of his passion. He rails
against the malice of the villagers in effecting a betrothal
which will frustrate his personal desires, and he promises a
bloody vengeance for the daring insult:

Yo iré en persona al monte,
Yo haré castigo en ellos de manera,
Que todo su horizonte
Arda con mi rigor, ¡Canalla fiera,
Bárbaros, viles, perros, atrevidos,
Perdiendo voy por Laura los sentidos! (III, vii).

These are the words of a man who has given himself totally over to his own passions. His wounded pride and his
frustration have caused him to forget completely all responsibility which he has as king to be dispassionate and mer-
ciful. He is reacting impulsively and he is blaming everyone involved for the frustration of his private desires. Unlike the Pedro of *La niña de plata* and *El médico de su honra*, whose angry outburst stemmed from a disappointment
with a trusted brother, this man is concerned with only
his own selfish pleasures and he has allowed his reason
and his self-control to be conquered by his unbridled passion.

Pedro enters the village with angry threats: «¡Quitad a

todos las vidas/ Sin que carbonero quede,/ y abrasad luego
sus casas!» (III, xvi). He tells his crossbowmen to kill
Bras and he orders Laura into his carriage. She begs for
mercy, and she reminds him of his promise never to harm
her. Hoping to distract him from his anger with the
villagers, she tells him that she has news of his half-sister.
This announcement has the desired effect of calming Pedro, and he demonstrates that his powers of reason have
been restored and freed from his passion when he resigns
himself to his loss of Laura and keeps his word to her not
to do her any injury.

As a matter of fact, Pedro demonstrates his sagacity
as well as his restored objectivity when he imposes the condition that Leonor marry one of his loyal subjects in order
to remove the threat which she poses to his official position.
Juan expresses his desire to marry her, and the play ends
on a note of harmony.

Although there are attempts in the play *La carbonera* to
defend the reputation of King Pedro as a wise and just
king, the actions of the man himself contradict much of
what is said in his defense. He is approaching a time of
crisis in his reign during which he will need to demonstrate
prudence and sound judgment in order to be able to regain
the support of those subjects who have rebelled against
him and joined his rival Enrique. If he continues to exhibit a lack of self-control he will confirm his reputation for
cruelty which, as we have seen in this play, is widespread
among his people.

Pedro's violent outbursts and vengefulness are rooted
in the increasing sense of insecurity from which he is suffering. This Pedro does not possess the quiet self-assurance
of the king of the *Audiencias*, who viewed the rebellion of
his half-brother as an inexplicable error in judgment on
the part of Enrique, which was doomed to failure. The
king of *La carbonera* feels persecuted by his half-brothers

and, although he is fearful of losing his crown, he does not concentrate his energy upon regaining the support of his people, but rather he alienates them further by his self-indulgence and his lack of consideration for them. He also lacks the support and companionship of the half-brothers who accompanied the king of *La niña de plata* and *El médico de su honra*, and he has grown suspicious of anyone who contradicts him even when he is in error.

Although Pedro exhibits similar characteristics in *Lo cierto por lo dudoso* and *La carbonera*, we must keep in mind the fact that while *Lo cierto por lo dudoso* is primarily a *comedia de enredo* in which Pedro appears as a *galán enamorado* with the conventional reactions of jealousy, melancholy and sentimentaly, in *La carbonera* there is some attempt to present him as a king as well as a man, and the fact that the effort to offset his reputation for cruelty results in something less than total success is indicative of a probable intention of the poet to suggest that Pedro is indeed a man capable of cruelty who may brng upon himself his own downfall if he does not learn to control his passions and regain the objectivity necessary for the proper execution of his office as king.

CHAPTER VI

CRISIS AND DOWNFALL

In *El rey don Pedro en Madrid* King Pedro is facing a crisis, the outcome of which will determine whether or not he will be able to maintain his position as King of Castilla. Since he has among his people a reputation for cruelty which has been published and nurtured by the contemporary *romances* and has gained widespread acceptance, it is important that he act in so exemplary a manner that he may by his own deeds demonstrate the injustice of the slander. The Infante Enrique poses a real threat to his position because of his popularity with the people and because of his contact with Pedro's political enemies.

Although King Pedro's suspicions of his half-brothers' activities are well-founded, Lope makes it clear in this play that he is not a totally innocent victim of their treachery as was the king of the *Audiencias*. As a man Pedro is guilty of an arrogance and a temerity which have caused him to forget the important matter of the salvation of his soul. By refusing to humble himself even in the face of compelling supernatural evidence of the power of divine vengeance, and by acting according to his desires and passions as a man rather than exercising self-control and reason, he is not fulfilling his duties as king.

136   FRANCES EXUM

Toward the end of the play, Pedro resolves to mend his
ways and try to save his soul and regain the support of his
people by pious deeds and exemplary justice. In *Los Ramírez de Arellano* we learn that he has not maintained this
resolution and that he has continued to allow his passions
to rule his will to such a degree that he has lost his divine
sanction to rule as King of Castilla. With his violent death
at Montiel at the hands of his victorious half-brother Enrique his downfall is complete.

In Act I of *El rey don Pedro en Madrid* Lope uses the
symbolism of Pedro's fall from a horse to show the immi-
ment danger of his downfall if he allows himself to be dominated by his passions. [1] His ferocious aspect in this
scene is described by the peasant Ginesa, who witnesses the
event as it takes place off-stage: «Fogoso, espumoso y fiero,/
A un bizarro caballero/ Un caballo ha descompuesto.»
(I, i). We hear the first words of Pedro from his position
off-stage, where he commits an unnecessary and violent act
as a release for his frustration: «Ya queda muerto el caballo!/ Que es la venganza mayor.» His use of the word
«vengeance» immediately informs the audience of his
suspicious and vengeful nature. The fact that his victim is
an innocent beast serves to emphasize the irrational nature
of his reaction. The combination of omen and violence set
the tone of sinister foreboding which pervades the entire
play.

Pedro enters with his unsheathed sword, which the peasant Elvira urges him to put away She offers him a place
to rest, but he is impatient to be on his way to Madrid,
and displays a single-purposed determination and an inner
tension which preclude his taking advantage of the offer
to enjoy a brief respite from his problems: «No hay cosa

---

[1] Lope also used this symbolism in *El médico de su honra*
and *Audiencias del rey don Pedro* to show the passionate «fall» of
Enrique and Leonardo, respectively.

en mí/ Que darme fatiga pueda.» (I, iii). This Pedro is a much more serious and tense individual than the king of *Ya anda la de Mazagatos* or even *La carbonera*, who enjoyed his diversion of the hunt because it gave him the opportunity to deal with the common people and forget his problems for a while.

Ginesa asks Pedro if he is one of the king's courtiers, and when he says that he is in the royal entourage on the way to Madrid, she asks him how he can hope to receive reward for his service to such a master as the king: «Porque cruel,/ Castilla a voces lo llama.» She remains adamant in her opinion, for when Pedro replies: «Su justicia el pueblo infama,» she insists: «La fama está en la opinión.» In an aside, Pedro takes careful note of this revelation of his reputation for cruelty, and he demonstrates that he considers it unfair. «¿Cruel es tu Rey, Castilla?/ Falso atributo le das.»

Aloud, he criticizes the malice of those who slander the king:

> Y ansí, miente el sedicioso
> Vulgo, que en él trueca fiero
> La parte de justiciero
> Que lo hace ilustre y glorioso. (I, ii).

Ginesa is obviously impressed by Pedro as a man, for she replies: «Si es tan bizarro y airoso/ El Rey como vos, no puede/ Ser cruel.» Anxious to be on his way, Pedro tells Busto to bring him a mount. He demonstrates generosity by giving him a costly ring. Busto reveals his love for Elvira by saying that such a rich stone is worthy of her, and the villagers begin to make ambiguous references to a problem which has prevented the marriage of the lovers. Elvira asks Pedro if the king would hear her complaint if she appealed to him directly, observing that: «Si es cruel, como le pintan,/ No hará de crueldades caso.» Pedro assures her that justice: «Es en él/ El atributo más alto.»

Elvira tells Pedro of the haughtiness and presumption of the Infanzón Tello:

> Deidad se hace de los montes
> Y majestad de los campos;
> Dueño en las vidas y haciendas,
> Poderoso, despreciando
> Con atrevimiento loco
> Los soberanos mandatos,
> No haciendo caso del Rey,
> Ni haciendo del cielo caso,
> Soberbio a lo poderoso,
> Y sacrílego a lo sacro,
> Al fin tirano, a quien tiemblan,
> Por lo altivo y por lo ingrato.
> El decoro en las doncellas
> Y el honor en los casados. (I, iii).

She tells of his violation of her, his violent attack on the villagers of Leganés who attempted to apprehend him, and his seizure of Leonor in Toledo on the eve of her wedding to Rodrigo. Pedro is angered at hearing of the arrogance of the Infanzón, who, in addition to tyrannizing his vassals, does not obey the laws of the king: «¡Que esté llena Castilla/ De reyes, cuando al propio no se humilla!»

Pedro's own pride is injured at the thought that one of his noblemen would be so disrespectful of his authority. He is jealous of his position, and he becomes steadily more enraged as he reviews the implications of the situation:

> ¿Quién infanzones son? ¿Quién ricoshombres?
> Caiga tanta cabeza;
> Sólo un cetro ha de haber, sólo una alteza;
> Que en los reinos del día,
> Sólo gobierna un sol la monarquía. (I, iii).

He asks where he may find this Tello, and he promises Elvira that he will see that Tello becomes her husband if she comes to Illescas to await him.

Forgetting his duties in Madrid and his desire to arrive at court as soon as possible, Pedro is now so curious about this man that he decides to go immediately to Illescas to judge for himself the character of the Infante. Ginesa observes that Tello has said that he is imitating his king in his violation of Leonor. Pedro is beside himself with rage at hearing such a statement: «¿Qué infanzoncillo es éste?/ Loco estoy, ¡vive Dios!» As he departs Pedro utters a threat which reflects his own pride in his position and his confidence in his ability to humble the proud Tello: «Hoy verá ese hombre loco/ Quién es la Majestad que tiene en poco.»

It is at this point that a mysterious *sombra* dressed in black makes its appearance and asks Pedro if he is the king. This *sombra* will appear three times, once in each act. He is much more than a mere dramatic device. An «alma en pena» who has not yet lost his human qualities, in his scenes with Pedro he attains the stature of a full-fledged dramatic character whose interaction with the king is as important to the action of the play as is the relationship between Pedro and the Infanzón Tello.

The vision claims to be «un hombre», and he tells Pedro not to be upset by his presence. The very suggestion that he might be afraid angers Pedro, and he exclaims that he is afraid of nothing: «Yo alterarme de un hombre,/ Cuando no hay imposible que me asombre!» (I, iv). The *sombra* goads him into an even stronger statement of his temerity by telling him to follow him, and then asking: «¿A seguirme te atreves?» Pedro replies: «Imagina/ Que soy don Pedro, y puedo/ Asegurarte que me tiembla el miedo.»

The fact that he refers to himself as Pedro, without reference to his position as king, demostrates his total confidence in his ability as an individual to be the master of this situation. The *sombra* has addressed him as king, but Pedro has chosen to answer as a man. The *sombra* shows

Pedro that he is superior to him by mounting the dead horse and flying away with the taunting query: «¿No me sigues?,» which leaves Pedro frustrated at not being able to follow. He accuses the *sombra* of cowardice in leaving him in this manner. The only answer that the vision gives him is that he will await him in Madrid.

Pedro does not dwell on the implications of his interview with the *sombra,* although he is aware that there has been a strong element of the supernatural about this strange «hombre». He dismisses the incident on the suspicion that it may have been a trick: «Todos son miedos vanos,/ Ilusiones de Blanca y mis hermanos.» This speech informs the audience that Pedro is on his guard against his half-brothers and he knows that he has reason to suppose that his aggrieved queen may join with them if given the opportunity.

The royal courtiers enter the stage and observe the emotional disturbance of their king. He tells them not to reveal his disguise. As Juan and Alonso remark on Pedro's valor, Fortún observes that there is something different in the king's manner: «Algo le ha sucedido.» (I, v). Having forgotten for the moment his meeting with the *sombra,* Pedro returns to his preoccupation with the Infanzón: «Ya me muero/ Por ver este infanzón bárbaro y fiero.»

In his first scene the Infanzón Tello proves to be every bit as arrogant and fearless as Elvira and Ginesa had said that he was. He boasts to Leonor and her father Fernando of his noble birth, claiming to be a descendant of Pelayo and equal to the kings of Castilla. He is no less proud of his own personal valor as an individual. Immediately following the long speech of Tello in which he tells of his power and importance, a servant enters with the news that «un bizarro caballero» has arrived and is waiting to see him. The timing of this arrival of King Pedro is as carefully calculated as was the appearance of the *sombra* to show that excessive pride and confidence will eventually lead to a down-fall.

Leonor confides to her father her hope that the new-comer may be Rodrigo, but she doubts that he would be so daring as to oppose the Infanzón. When the servant asks if he should have the man enter, Tello replies: «¿Cuándo mi casa/ Se impide a nadie?» (I, vii). This statement has the familiar ring of the response characteristic of King Pedro when asked if he will receive his subjects for the *audiencias*. This fact, coupled with the overweening pride that Tello has expressed in his noble birth and his personal valor reveal that he shares many of the characteristics of his king, and suggests that we should perhaps expect a par-allel between this character and that of King Pedro. [2]

Tello orders Leonor and Fernando to be seated and he seats himself in the only other chair available, boasting ironically: «Que yo sentado recibo/ Al mismo Rey.» (I, vii). As Pedro enters, both Tello and Fernando remark on his noble appearance. Pedro is insulted by the fact that Tello has received him in this arrogant manner, but he resolves to restrain his anger and maintain his disguise in order to be able to fashion an awesome vengeance which may serve as an example to other presumptuous noblemen:

> ¡Sentado se está el grosero!
> Por hacer que ruede estoy,
> De un puntapié, hasta el infierno;
> Pero si aquí le castigo,
> Con su muerte no escarmiento
> Los tiranos de Castilla,
> Que han de temblar en su ejemplo. (I, viii).

Without taking off his hat, Pedro asks to kiss the hands

---

[2] Sister Rosario María Asturias noted this fact in her critical edition of the play, and we are indebted to her for her many astute observations.

of his host. Testing his visitor, Tello replies curtly: «Des-cubierto/ No he de oille.» In a play on words, Pedro in-forms Tello that since he has not revealed his identity, his nobility is not «descubierto.» The Infanzón recognizes both the apparently high social status and the astuteness of the man. He has a stool brought for Pedro to sit upon, saying: «Dos sillas tengo,/ Que son la que ocupo yo/ Y la que ocupa mi suegro.» Fernando immediately offers Pedro his own chair, but Pedro refuses: «La ley alterar no quiero/ Que se usa con los demás.»

Tello's impudent reply reflects the true historical situa-tion of fourteenth-century Castilla in which the power of the crown had not yet been consolidated and the king was still plagued by rebellions on the part of powerful indivi-duals: «Los infanzones del reino,/ Apenas dan silla al Rey/ En sus casas.» In a aside Pedro angrily denounces his advisers for not keeping him better informed of the treachery of such men as Tello: «Todos me engañan, y ansí/ Me llama el Cruel el pueblo.»

When Tello inquires as to the specific level of nobility of his guest, Pedro claims to be a member of the Acebedo family of Córdoba. Tello seems satisfied of his nobility, and he asks what his business is in Toledo. Pedro replies: «Al Rey me hacen seguir pleitos.» Tello calls such expen-sive legal maneuvering absurd when one may settle his dis-putes with a sword. When Pedro observes: «La ley se ha de obedecer,» Tello impudently states that he obeys only God's law.

Containing his anger, Pedro warns him: «Ya al Rey en Madrid tenemos.» Tello scornfully replies: «Vendrá con doña María/ A darnos cristiano ejemplo.» This mention of his illicit affair with María de Padilla brings Pedro to his feet in a defense of her reputation:

> Ya es nuestra Reina y señora
> Y su legítimo empleo,
> Y al que no hablare en sus partes
> Con decoro y con respeto,
> ¡Vive Dios que... (I, viii).[3]

Tello calms his guest and observes: «Mucho quiere al Rey.»
Pedro replies simply and significantly: «Es Rey.» Undaunted, Tello continues to insult the reputation of the king and to assert his own importance by stating that he has served as host to King Alfonso, Pedro's own father: «Cuyos gloriosos trofeos/ Hoy el rey don Pedro infama.»

Pedro's next speech of warning to Tello reveals the fact that he realizes that as a man he is not overly endowed with tolerance, but that he strives to maintain the self-control required of his office:

> Hablad bien del rey don Pedro:
> Advertid que es mal sufrido,
> Y que es rey, y que a no serlo,
> Os echara a puntapiés
> Y a coces de aqueste asiento. (I, viii).

Almost succumbing to his impulse to fulfil his verbal threat, Pedro moves menacingly toward the Infanzón. Tello is amazed at his belligerent attitude, but he excuses his show of hostility: «Que le disculpe el buen celo/ De su Rey.» Pedro agrees: «Soy buen vasallo,/ ¡Vive Dios!» Tello reproves him for his needless swearing and observes again how much he loves his king. Pedro repeats his earlier simple and meaningful reply, which has an ominous ring to it in this tense situation: «Es rey.»

Pedro realizes that he has acted rashly in threatening violence, and he apologizes: «Perdonad, que éstos han sido,/

---

[3] This claim of a legitimate marriage is contrary to historical fact, although Pedro did claim María as his legitimate queen after her death at the *Cortes* in Sevilla (1362).

Señor, fogosos afectos/ De vasallo.» Although Tello insists
that he, too, is a loyal vassal of the king, Pedro warns him
once again to speak more respectfully of God's representative on earth. Pedro prods Tello to reveal the full extent of
his presumption by telling him that he has heard of the
power and influence that he has in his local area: «Dicen
que en ella/ Con el Rey partís el cetro.» Flattered, Tello
admits that even the king's decrees must have his approval
before being published in the area under his control. Hearing this, Pedro can hardly resist the temptation to reveal
his identity and chastise Tello, but he restrains himself,
realizing that he may better serve the cause of justice by
maintaining his disguise and biding his time. Once again
he expresses his determination to make an awesome example of his judgment of the Infanzón:

> Que en otra ocasión pretendo
> Ilustrar con este loco
> El blasón de justiciero;
> Y si aquí a coces le mato,
> Mi misma justicia ofendo,
> Y me infamo. (I, viii).

Pedro's own suggestion that he would be capable of
killing Tello in such a brutal manner gives the audience
insight into a deep-rooted tendency to violence in his nature
which does not appear on the surface.

When Elvira and Ginesa burst into the room and confront Tello with his crime he does not deny that he has
willfully dishonored Elvira, and he coldly asks her what
she intends to do about it. She replies that she intends
to prevent him from marrying Leonor since he has interfered
with her marriage to Busto. Tello again challenges the
power of the king as he says that he will marry Leonor in
defiance of the king and «todo el poder del suelo.» (I, ix).

It is highly significant that he limits himself to a defiance of earthly authority.

This statement, combined with his earlier assertion that he obeys divine law and his reproval of Pedro's use of God's name in an oath demonstrate clearly that although Tello may be a presumptuous rebel against human law, he is fully cognizant of the necessity for humility and submission before God. As we shall see, this is one outstanding difference between Tello and Pedro as men.

Pedro once again restrains himself from punishing the arrogance of Tello only by dint of supreme effort, and he observes bitterly in an aside: «Y después dicen que soy/ Mal sufrido!» His next words are fraught with dramatic irony: «Mas el tiempo/ Llegará de su castigo.» Punishment will come also in time to King Pedro if he disobeys the law of God.

When Tello thinks to make amends for his crime by offering to contribute to the dowry of Elvira, Pedro pretends to find this a reasonable reparation in order to elicit Elvira's threat to take her complaint directly to the king. Tello again expresses his scorn for King Pedro:

> ¿Con el Rey me amenazáis?
> El Rey podrá, por lo excelso
> De la majestad, mandallo;
> Pero yo no obedecello.
> Y cuando me lo mandara,
> En el campo cuerpo a cuerpo,
> Sin majestad, yo le hiciera
> Que lo heroico de mi pecho
> Conociera a cuchilladas. (I, ix).

He adds that often it is more the political power of a king than his worth as a man which is respected and feared, and he scorns Pedro's killing of «un músico» and «un clérigo de Evangelio.» Pedro calmly observes: «Todos son hombres.»

As all are preparing to leave, Tello postpones the wedding celebrations, observing: «Que es todo azares y agüeros.» He shows that he has been pleased by Pedro as a man when he invites him to remain. Pedro's final words of Act I are an aside in which he makes another threat to show «este necio» the power of King Pedro in Madrid.

This long scene between Pedro and Tello closely parallels the conversation between Pedro and the *sombra*, since in each case the party seeking the interview pretends to hold a less important position than he in fact possesses, and in both situations he is seeking to determine the extent of the presumption and the degree of guilt of the man interviewed.

The whole first act is carefully designed to reveal four distinct levels of power and self-assertion. The least aggressive character is Rodrigo, who made no effort to prevent Tello from carrying off his bride Leonor. The Infanzón is presumptuous and scornful of human law, but he claims to respect divine authority. Pedro defies even the unknown in his aggressive assertion of his personal valor. The *sombra* itself displays human characteristics in that he seems to enjoy taunting Pedro into ever more rash statements and in frustrating his attempts to follow him. Since as an «alma en pena» he is not yet completely removed from the human sphere and yet he participates in the divine, and will serve as a symbol of divine justice, he may be considered as a legitimate dramatic character and as such occupy the highest level of authority in the play.

Act II opens with the arrival of aggrieved subjects at an *audiencia* of King Pedro. An alférez who has served his king well for twenty years comes face-to-face with Pedro for the first time. The majesty of the king leaves the man awe-stricken and speechless. Pedro rewards his service by promoting him to the rank of captain. He then decides to test for himself the valor of his soldier. He offers him his hand, applying pressure until the man becomes angered and, forgetting that he is addressing the king, he threatens Pedro. Pedro orders a generous monetary reward for such spirit and he says with satisfaction: «Ansí/ Quiero los soldados yo.» (II, ii). The soldier echoes his sentiment: «Y yo ansí a los reyes quiero/ ¡Vive Dios!» Pedro states that his reason for this action is to assure that he commands the respect of his soldiers: «Esto/ Es porque en facción o en puesto/ Veais la mano que os di.»

This attitude is similar to the one displayed by the king of *El médico de su honra* who, after testing the personal worth of Jacinto, displayed his desire to command the respect of such a valiant subject. Pedro expresses satisfaction at being able to reward the loyal service of the *alférez*, and he observes: «Es desdichado el rey/ A quien no aman sus soldados.»

In the next case which comes before him, Pedro shows contempt for useless officials who serve only to complicate the administration of the realm and do not have the interest of the common people at heart. He forces a *contador* to lay aside a carefully-worded *memorial* and speak directly to him in petitioning to remain in his service as a manager of the royal accounts. He then rejects the plea, saying: «Rey que recibe y paga,/ No ha menester Contadores.» (II, ii).

In like manner, when presented with an *arbitrio* which is said to concern the welfare of the people, Pedro tears it to pieces without reading it and says that he will discharge the matter personally: «Que no hay arbitrio que sea/ En favor de los vasallos.» This attitude of distrust toward technically-worded documents and involved legal maneuvers must been appreciated by the Spanish Golden Age audience, which so thoroughly enjoyed criticism directed against scribes and lawyers, and must have felt a warmth of kinship with this aggressive king who insisted upon dealing directly with the problems of his people.

The next subject to enter the royal *audiencia* is Clarindo,[4] who claims to be a poet. Pedro welcomes him: «Pues animad y escribid,/ Que en mí tienen premio igual/ Armas y letras.» In a bit of advice worthy of the idol of the *vulgo*, Lope de Vega, Pedro instructs him to please the people if he wants to achieve success.

In this scene of the *audiencias* of King Pedro, Lope presents Pedro as a conscientious *rey justiciero* similar to the king of the *Audiencias*, a fact which has caused one recent critic of the drama to conclude that this play is mainly an attempt to rehabilitate the reputation of Pedro I.[5] Although Pedro does appear with his virtues as well as his vices in this drama, in the opinion of the present writer there is no basis for considering the play an apology for the monarch, since the poet clearly demonstrates the errors by which King Pedro will bring upon himself the loss of his crown.

Leonor and Tello arrive at the palace, where the peasant girls of Leganés are dressed in courtly attire and are awaiting the king's summons. Ginesa fears the king's reputed cruelty, while Elvira is confident that he will marry her to Tello. Both girls wonder where the dashing courtier they had met in Leganés may be, and they praise his eloquence and nobility, observing that he had befriended the Infanzón. Meanwhile, Pedro is savoring his anticipation of the humbling of the Infanzón: «Hoy verá el poder que alcanza/ Este grosero, este loco,/ Que tiene a mi cetro en poco.»

In contrast to his efforts to reduce the presumption of

---

[4]   Since Clarindo is the literary disguise of Andrés de Claramonte, who is thought by most critics to have reworked the original play, this scene may be one of his changes.

[5]   Sandra Lou Brown, «Tirso de Molina: His Treatment of Medieval Spanish History» (Unpublished doctoral dissertation, University of North Carolina, Chapel Hill, 1969), p. 197.

Tello, Pedro tries to increase the aggressiveness of the rather passive Rodrigo, who comes to him seeking justice for
the abduction of his bride Leonor. He speaks to Rodrigo
as a friend as well as king, carefully distinguishing between
the advice he offers as a man and the duty he must fulfil as
king:

> Mi ley
> Temed, y haced lo que os digo,
> Que uno es consejo de amigo,
> Y otro advertencia de rey. (II, iii).

Still hesitant, Rodrigo asks if he dare to confront Tello in the
palace itself. Pedro's reply reflects both his personal opinion
as a man and his official position as king: «Don Pedro os
dice que sí,/ Y el rey don Pedro que no».

Tello is insulted that he is not allowed entry by way of
the main entrance. He tries to leave, but is detained, and
when he complains of being held against his will, his companion Cordero observes: «Si conoces al Rey, ¿para qué
entraste?» (II, vii). This statement reveals that Pedro's
reputation for severity is also shared by the people at the
courts of the nobles. Angry and frustrated at being a captive of the king, Tello asserts his valor and reaffirms his
nobility in a verbal tirade:

> ¿Qué es coger? Mi espada es ésta,
> De quien aun tiembla Castilla,
> Y de quien los reyes tiemblan.
> Ricohombre soy e Infanzón,
> Y a la par de sí me asienta
> El Conde de Trastamara,
> Que es su hermano. (II, viii).

As soon as he has uttered these defiant words, Rodrigo,
acting on the advice of Pedro, confronts him, and the two
men are taken into custody for drawing their swords in the
royal palace. Tello is humiliated by the incident: «¡Que

se atreva/ Un escudero a un ricohombre,/ Y que el Rey se
lo consienta!» He vents his wrath and frustration on Leonor, saying that he no longer wants to marry her. As the
two men are taken from the room Rodrigo expresses his
satisfaction to Leonor: «Esto es ser rey./ Alegre vas».
(II, x). Cordero observes that King Pedro has caught the
Infanzón like a mouse in a trap, and Tello reveals his frustration in an oath similar to the one for which he had
criticized Pedro in Act I: «No hay sino tener paciencia./
¡Vive Dios!»

When summoned to what he believes will be the presence of King Pedro, Tello is still defiant and self-confident,
but the courtier Juan observes: «El saldrá sin soberbia,/
Que es, si él arrogante y loco,/ Temerario el que lo espera» (II, xi). Tello and Cordero are not taken directly into
the presence of the king, but rather into another empty
room in which they must again wait. This psychological
technique of anticipation and disappointment wears down
the patience and undermines the confidence of the proud
Infanzón. [6] When Cordero asks: «¿Qué intenta este Rey?»
(II, xii). Tello shows his anger with an emotional outburst
and another oath: «Intenta/ Irritarme e irritar/ La caste-
llana nobleza;/ Y ¡vive Dios!». This speech of Tello reflects
once again the situation of the Castilian Crown in the fourteenth century. Tello is only one of many rebellious noblemen whom Pedro is seeking to intimidate in the hope
of being able to assure peace in his kingdom and to esta-
blish the political stability of the monarchy.

Cordero admonishes Tello to control his irritation, since
as hostile prisoners in an atmosphere in which no one is
secure in his position they are at a great disadvantage.

---

[6] I. L. McClelland demonstrates how this dramatic suspense
reveals the inner fears in the mind of Tello and she suggests that
the dramatist intended in this manner to reveal also the inner fears
of King Pedro himself.

He comments on the sense of unreality which their isolation has bred in him and he feels the menace of the power of the Castilian Crown as a disembodied reality apart from the person of the king: «¿Si es duende el Rey?» (II, xii). Both men feel even more strongly the oppressive weight of suspense of the king's imminent vengeance when Elvira enters the room, crosses in silence, and exits without even glancing in their direction. Tello exclaims: «¡Qué necio he sido en fiarme/ Del Rey!» The completely intimidated Cordero observes that no place in the realm would offer security from the vengeance of this all-pervasive authority.

Lope combines in these scenes a realistic picture of the instability of the political atmosphere of fourteenth-century Castilla with a presentation of the concept of the «king's two bodies». Cordero and Tello comment upon the individual character of the mortal man Pedro as a severe ruler at the same time that they sense the almost supernatural aura which surrounds the mystical body of the king and pervades the very atmosphere even in the absence of the man himself.

The courtier Alonso comes to take the two men from this room into yet another empty chamber, and he notes the profound psychological effect that the suspense of waiting has had on Tello: «La fiereza / Deste Infanzón jabalí/ El Rey desta suerte templa.» (II, xiv). Tello has become aware of the awesome oppression of the abstract power of the Crown, and he realizes that this special aura surrounding the royal Majesty is a supernatural quality to be respected and feared:

> Esta majestad que ves,
> Es la que los hombres tiemblan;
> Que por sí solos son hombres
> Los reyes, mas la grandeza
> Los pasa a divinidades. (II, xv).

In this clear expression of the dichotomy of the king's body politic and his body natural Tello admits that he has come to understand that he has been in error to criticize the purely human side of the king and ignore the divine power with which he is also invested. He admits that he fears the almost tangible Majesty of King Pedro.

Taken to yet another empty waiting room, Tello expresses his frustration at his impotence against the abstract power which menaces them.

As the door opens, he expresses his dread of the meeting with King Pedro. He admits that he has been conquered psychologically by the Majesty of the king: «Ya soy de piedra: / ¡Tan valiente es en su casa / Un rey!» (II, xvii). When he recognizes Pedro as being the man who had been in his home the day before, Tello is so fearful that he kneels silently to await the king's recognition of his presence. Pedro, who is reading a letter, does not deign to lift his eyes from the page in order to acknowledge Tello's respectful greeting. Cordero reminds his master of his own reception of Pedro in Illescas, mimicking his manner: «En mi casa aún no se sientan / Los reyes: dos sillas tengo.» He observes that Pedro is avenging himself «lindamente» for the treatment he received at Tello's home. Although Pedro does acknowledge the presence of Tello, at first he does not give him his complete attention, but interjects comments to his servants concerning the answer to be sent to the letter that he has been reading.

Finally he concentrates both his attention and the full fury of his anger upon the person of the Infanzón. Pedro's own pride in his manly prowess is evident in his threat to humble Tello's presumption:

> Yo el Rey soy, porque nací
> De tan soberana esfera,
> Que cuando rey no naciera,
> Lo pudiera ser por mí.

> Yo en la campaña y aquí
> Si medimos espadas,
> Os daré las cuchilladas
> Que darme ese brazo intenta. (II, xxiii).

These words are almost identical to those uttered by Tello in Act I, and Lope's intended parallel between Pedro and Tello is again obvious. After he vents his scorn by knocking Tello's head against the wall, Pedro stalks out of the room, leaving the humiliated Infanzón to the dubious consolation of Cordero's reminder that such treatment at the hands of a king is not so injurious to one's honor as an insult by an ordinary man.

Elvira and Leonor are brought into the room to confront Tello with his crimes. Elvira reminds him of the certainty of divine justice. Her choice of words clearly indicates that she is addressing Tello as the author of not only his own crimes, but also as the symbol of the sins of King Pedro himself:

> Y ansí te previene
> Leyes que te ofusquen,
> Iras que te espanten,
> Muertes que te turben,
> Sombras que te cerquen,
> Ansias que te apuren,
> Sierpes que te muerdan,
> Hombres que te acusen,
> Culpas que te venzan,
> Varas que te juzguen,
> Y almas ofendidas
> Que tu muerte anuncien. (II, xx).

It is Pedro who is receiving the visits of the *sombra* and who will hear the prophecy of his own death from the «alma» of one of his own victims.

Alone with his courtiers, Pedro hears a ballad which Clarindo has composed which tells of his fall from the horse and his meeting with Elvira and Ginesa. The king marvels at the rapidity with which news of his activities is transmitted by song throughout the kingdom. This reference to the contemporary ballads of Pedro's reign adds yet another note of authenticity to the fourteenth-century setting of the play.

Pedro is restless, and he asks that the song be discontinued for the present. He decides to go out in disguise to «rondar,» but changes his mind when he finds the night too calm for his liking. He then asks that books be brought to him so that he may divert himself from his inability to console himself in demonstrations of valor by reading of the famous deeds of Casar.

No sooner has he made this decision than he immediately changes his mind and calls for dueling swords. When Alfonso observes that no one will be willing to oppose him out of respect for his position, Pedro complains of the corresponding respect that he wishes to earn as a man but which is denied him: «Que me veneráis por rey,/ y no me teméis por mí.» He reveals his need for reassurance of his worth as an individual and he complains bitterly of the restrictions of his office:

> Poco hombre debo de ser.
> ¡Qué desdichado nací
> En nacer rey, pues no puedo
> Por mis acciones lucir! (II, xxiv).

Once again we see the insecurity of Pedro as a man which we observed in *Lo cierto por lo dudoso* and *La carbonera*.

Only one of his courtiers, Fortún, dares to actually oppose the king in a contest of skill at swordsmanship. Just as he had done in his earlier scene with the spirited alférez, Pedro, after succeding in wounding Fortún slightly, rewards him richly for his bravery. The other courtiers exit one by one, refusing to heed the command of Pedro to each in his turn to take a sword and oppose him on a man-to-man basis.

At this psychologically propitious moment the *sombra* appears for the second time, answering Pedro's command to the retreating courtiers to take up «la espada» with the words: «Ya estoy aquí/ Y la tomaré contigo.» (II, xxv). In an approach similar to the one employed by Pedro with the Infanzón, the *sombra* asks the king if he knows whom he is addressing. Stil scornful and unafraid, Pedro replies: «Eres una forma vil/ Del infierno.» The *sombra* is again taunting Pedro with the possibility of being able to test his prowess against him, and the furious king is frustrated anew by the impossibility of coming to blows with his mocking challenger: «No hallo cuerpo que ofenderte,/ Aunque veo la forma en ti.»

Pedro's frustration in this scene parallels that of Tello, when, alone in the waiting-room with Cordero, he was longing to be able to confront the abstraction which was theatening him and defeat it by his skill as a swordsman. The *sombra* goads Pedro by telling him that it is he who must retreat from this encounter. Believing that the vision is testing him in the same manner that he had just tested his own courtiers, Pedro angrily replies: «Aquí tengo de matarte,/ Aunque no puedas morir.»

Satisfied of Pedro's temerity even in the face of the unknown, the *sombra* observes cryptically: «Pues con todo ese valor,/ Has de ser piedra en Madrid.» He extinguishes the light, leaving Pedro in total darkness and frustration. Pedro again accuses the *sombra* of cowardice for refusing to fight him, and he threatens to follow him even into the darkness of Hell itself, which he which he will cause to tremble for fear of his fury.

The organization of the scenes of Act II is calculated to reinforce the contrast between the four levels of aggressiveness and authority represented by Rodrigo, Tello, Pedro and the *sombra*. The king encourages Rodrigo to assert himself against Tello, dealing the first blow to the pride of the Infanzón. Then, in the carefully-planned strategy of prolonging the suspense of this meeting with Tello, Pedro succeeds in the psychological defeat of his rival by making him aware of his superiority over him as king.

Later, as Pedro is plagued by doubts as to his own superiority as an individual and is seeking to prove his valor against his reluctant courtiers, the appearance of the *sombra*, with his obvious intention of testing the temerity of the king and his psychologically effective technique of leaving Pedro in suspense as to the meaning of his words, parallels closely the treatment which Pedro had used to humble Tello.

It is now clear that the mission of the *sombra* is to humble the pride of Pedro. The effective use of dramatic suspense in Lope's portrayal of the mental anguish of both Tello and Pedro shifts the emphasis of this act from the usual level of mere physical action involving the protagonists of a Spanish Golden Age *comedia* and lifts the relationship between Tello and Pedro and that of Pedro and the *sombra* to an abstract place on which it is their psychological interaction which predominates.

In Act III Leonor decides to petition the king to show mercy toward the Infanzón despite the seriousness of his crimes. As Pedro enters it is clear that he has been shaken by the second visit of the *sombra*, for he is pondering his enigmatic prediction: «¿Piedra he de ser? ¡Hola, hola!» (III, i). He is so distracted and preoccupied by his thoughts of the *sombra* that he seems unaware of the presence of his courtiers. Finally conquering his doubts with the vain rationalization that the prophecy must be a trick devised by his ambitious half-brothers, he reasserts himself by uttering a series of threats against them, swearing to humble the pretensions of Enrique when he arrives at the palace.

In this aggressive and vengeful frame of mind Pedro is not receptive to the pleas of clemency for Tello, and he rails at Leonor and Elvira for attempting to interfere with his justice. He reveals the extent of his severity by ordering the execution of not only Tello but also Rodrigo, and he makes the following statement of his reasons:

> El rey que agravios perdona
> Hechos a la Majestad,
> Se agravia a sí, porque consta
> Ansí de justicia el cetro
> Como de misericordia;
> Y éstas han de ser iguales,
> Que una falta, si otra sobra. (III, ii).

No sooner has he uttered these words for the benefit of the peasant girls and Leonor than he reveals to one of his courtiers his preoccupation with testing for himself the valor of Tello. He states his intention to «rondar», since the night has the sinister and stormy aspect which he prefers as an aid to his disguise. His reasons for this custom are the same in this play as they were in *El médico de su honra*: a combination of a quest for adventure and a desire to know the truth about his reputation among his people.

> De los reyes
> Son aforismos las rondas.
> La noche, lo que hay, me dice,
> En el pueblo; que en sus sombras
> Y en su silencio y espanto
> No se acreditan lisonjas. (III, iii).

Pedro has arranged with Alonso to have Tello released so that he may confront him man-to-man and discover if he is superior to the Infanzón as an individual as well as in his official position as king. Pedro admonishes Alonso to guard closely his secret: «Mira cuan breve distancia/

Hay del infierno a la gloria.» These words are especially significant, since Pedro's own temerity in defying the unknown in the person of the *sombra* endangers his soul as well as his life.

Alonso arranges for Tello to be confessed by a priest before he comes and takes away the light so that the men will not recognize King Pedro. As he is taking the lamp, Cordero begs him not to leave them in darkness: «Que es azar morir a obscuras:/ Mueran, señor, a obscuras los herejes.» (III, v). This mention of confession, darkness and heresy which follows so closely the remarks of Pedro about the glory one may gain even in the process of assuring his own damnation, forms a parallel of symbolism with the second scene between Pedro and the *sombra* in which the latter twice extinguished Pedro's light and caused him to threaten to follow him even in the darkness of heretical defiance of divine authority.

Clearly Lope is suggesting that if Pedro does not learn to control his passionate nature and recognize a higher authority than his own he will be in danger of incurring the most severe penalty of divine justice: the damnation of his soul.

Pedro arrives in disguise at the cell of the Infanzón and tells Cordero that he comes as a friend to free Tello from the cruelty of the king. To Tello's question: «¿Qué del Rey me escapáis?» he replies: «Seguid lo obscuro,/ Y pensad que conmigo vais seguro.» (III, vii). These words are heavily laden with dramatic irony, for the darkness symbolizes the blind passion which is causing Pedro as a man insecure in his own estimation of himself to force a confrontation with Tello, breaking in the process his own law by helping a prisoner guilty of high treason to escape. Tello will be far from «safe» in his company, for Pedro plans to exercise every effort to kill him in their duel in order to reassure himself of his superiority as a man.

The use of darkness as a symbol of the error which is committed by Pedro in allowing himself to be controlled by his passions is once again reminiscent of the scene with the *sombra* when Pedro rashly theatened to brave the total darkness of Hell, if necessary, in order to assert himself against the scorn of the vision.

The Infante Enrique and his companion Mendoza arrive at the walls of the palace and decide to await daylight to enter. Mendoza expresses fear of the king's power and envy of Enrique. Enrique reveals that he enjoys the peace of mind one who has a clear conscience. He tries to calm Mendoza's fears. In view of the increasing preoccupation of King Pedro with «ilusiones vanos» occasioned by the *sombra*, these complacent words of the calm and self-possessed Enrique demonstrate the contrast evident in the present psychological state of the two brothers.

In a demonstration of his virtue and good intentions, Enrique becomes angered by the suspicions of Mendoza concerning the king's vengefulness toward him. He warns Mendoza not to criticize God's representative on earth and not to question the king's justice, which, after all, is an extension of the often inscrutable justice of God:

> Y ansí, en quebrar esta ley,
> Vete, Mendoza, a la mano;
> Que es ofenderme cn mi hermano,
> Y es irritarme en mi rey. (III, viii).

This attitude of total trust and brotherly afection on the part of Enrique contrasts sharply with the caution and vengefulness which Pedro has demonstrated toward his half-brother. Like the king of Act III of *El médico de su honra* this King Pedro has come to suspect the ambition of Enrique.

Just as Enrique and Mendoza are taking a rest from their journey, an ominous prophecy is heard in the form of

a popular *romance* which is sung by a group of children
off-stage:

> Muchachitos de Madrid,
> Del rey don Pedro os guardad;
> Que quien mata al Infanzón,
> Sus hermanos matará. (III, viii).

Mendoza is startled, and Enrique tries to calm him with
the ironical observation: «Que es/ Voz de Dios querrás de-
cir.» Mendoza agrees that the song may indeed be a divine
warning to Enrique. Although Enrique refuses to be influenced by the prophetic overtone of the song, he is curious
about the news that it offers of the king's dispute with an
Infanzón. Mendoza makes an observation which is reminiscent of the satirical remarks of Galindo in *El médico de
su honra* when he says that no bit of news escapes a diligent
court chronicler.

When Pedro suggests to Tello that they pause in their
flight from his prison, the Infanzón reveals the extent of
his new-found respect for the Majesty of the king: «Mas
adelante pasemos;/ Que temo al Rey.» However, Tello adds
that his respect does not include fear of the king as a man:

> Pero yo se le pusiera,
> A batallar cuerpo a cuerpo
> Y hombre a hombre donde estamos;
> Que aquí no importa el respeto. (III, ix).

Promising to provide money, letters of safe conduct and
horses to the men for their escape to Aragón, Pedro sends
Cordero to a nearby house for a lamp. He then pretends
to hear a noise which suggests the presence of an unidenti-
fied man who is spying on them and, giving Tello a sword,
he suggests that they separate and accost the intruder. Tello promises ironically: «Guardaré la vida y puesto/ Del
Rey mismo.» (III, x).

Pedro returns immediately in his new disguise as the intruder to test the valor of Tello: «Agora ha de ver si en mí/ Triunfa el valor o el respeto.» When he succeeds in conquering Tello in the the ensuing struggle, Pedro is satisfied of his own worth:

> Hombre soy...
> (Y he deseado sabello),
> Hombre soy que por diez valgo,
> Pues que contigo peleo
> Aquí, que vales por tantos;
> Y ansí, en ti diez hombres venzo. (III, x).

Defeated physically, Tello is humiliated and prefers death to the king's knowledge of his shame. Pedro, savoring his victory, compels Tello to admit that he has proven to be the better man:

> Confiesa que por mí solo
> Ser respetado merezco
> Tanto como el Rey por ser
> Rey; y confiesa que puedo
> Por mi bizarría más
> Que el Rey por su nacimiento;
> Y, al fin, confiesa que aquí
> Entre las plantas te tengo. (III, x).

When Cordero brings the lamp and Tello sees that it is the king who has defeated him, Pedro tells him that he is satisfied with his past victories over him and that he will allow him to escape further punishment:

> Pues ya
> Que has visto que reñir puedo
> Contigo en campaña, y sabes
> Que por mí mismo te venzo,
> Y no por la majestad
> Ni el soberano respeto;
> Y sabes que te vencí
> En tu casa por modesto,

> Y en mi palacio por rey;
> Y en estos tres vencimientos
> Me has admirado piadoso,
> Témeme por justiciero,
> Y véte, pues estás libre,
> De Castilla y destos reinos,
> Porque si en ellos te hallo
> Has de morir sin remedio;
> Que aquí la espada te libra,
> Y allí te amenaza el cetro. (III, xi).

Once again, in a scene similar to his earlier one with Rodrigo, the king-man dichotomy of Pedro is revealed, as he
acts as a friend in freeing Tello and at the same time warns
him that he may expect stern justice of him in his role as
king if he does not succeed in escaping. Tello, in awe of
Pedro both as king and as man, and conquered both physically and psychologically, admits his humility: «Que allá
me venciste Rey,/ Y aquí me vences don Pedro.»

Now at the height of his glory both as king and as man,
Pedro is about to go to rest from his activities when the
sombra makes his third and final appearance. It is in
this interview, which Menéndez y Pelayo considers the least
effective of the three, [7] that the *sombra* reveals his identity
to Pedro and succeeds in humbling the proud spirit of the
king in much the same manner that Pedro has just humbled
the Infanzón.

The loquaciousness of the ghost which Menéndez y Pelayo criticizes serves to heighten his effectiveness as a
dramatic character. He has been sent as a divine emissary
to direct Pedro to make a contribution to the Church in reparation for his sin in having killed one of God's creatures,
but he cannot resist talking about himself a bit more than
is necessary to his purpose. He begins by inviting Pedro to
sit down, and the scene acquires the aspect of a conversation

---

[7]   Menéndez y Pelayo, *Estudios*, IV, 345.

between two ordinary men, one of whom is impatient to be rid of his tiresome companion.

When Pedro starts to leave, the *sombra* employs the same completely human method for regaining his full attention which Pedro had tried with him on previous occasions: he accuses him of cowardice. Once Pedro is again seated, the *sombra*, instead of stating his mission succintly, begins by repeating his question to Pedro concerning whether or not he has recognized him. Pedro, tired of the lengthy preliminaries, repeats his belief that he is a demon who is pursuing him, and he starts to leave once again.

Indicating that he is about to come to his point, the *sombra* tells Pedro that he is the spirit of a priest whom Pedro had killed outside of the Convent of San Clemente in Sevilla. He elaborates further by saying that he was about to say mass when the event took place. Pedro, intrigued at this disclosure, asks him about his status and learns that the man was a deacon.

The *sombra* emphasizes the fact that he was an important man, that his death was a great sacrilege. He asks Pedro if he remembers the details of the incident. He reminds him that he had been attempting to kidnap a lady named Beatriz from the convent, and that the murder had been the result of his own efforts to restrain the overamorous king. Pedro observes that love is indeed a cruel passion which robs men of their reason. The conversation has now taken on the aspect of a discussion between a live priest and a rather philosophical but as yet unrepentant sinner.

The *sombra* then takes Pedro's dagger in his hand and says that it will be the very weapon with which Enrique will kill him if he does not repent of his sins and mend his ways. At the mention of Enrique, Pedro becomes enraged, and he fearlessly tells the *sombra* that he would kill him again if it were possible. Still in no hurry to tell Pedro the reason for his mission, the *sombra* does not

reveal his business until Pedro interrupts him to ask:
«¿Qué es tu intento?» (III, xiii). Thus pressed, the *sombra* explains his prior statement that Pedro will be «piedra en Madrid» by telling the king that it is God's will that he found a convent in Madrid. He reveals his personal interest in the gesture: «Y advierte que ansí me sacas/ De las penas que padezco.»

When Pedro inquires about his suffering, the *sombra* asks him to take his hand so that he may feel the fire that is burning within him. When Pedro can no longer stand the heat of the handclasp, the *sombra*, satisfied that Pedro has thus gained some idea of the anguish that he is undergoing, loosens his grasp, and says simply: «Este es el fuego que paso.» [8] This handclasp may be viewed as a further test of Pedro's temerity and determination, since this action is similar to the one which Pedro employed to test the valor of the *alférez*.

Pedro is humbled as he feels in his grasp the full fury of divine retribution. Having thus tested Pedro's valor and having humbled the presumption of the proud king, the *sombra* warns Pedro that he, too, must learn fear: the fear of the torments of Hell. When he disappears, Pedro is left in awe of the unknown forces which have sent a warning to him in the guise of the spirit of one of his victims.

Physically undefeated, but conquered psychologically by the certainty of his eternal punishment if he does not show greater respect for divine authority, Pedro resolves to do as bidden by the *sombra*:

> Luego he de labrar el templo,
> Porque por él se revoquen
> Los soberanos decretos,
> Y esta advertencia le deba
> A Madrid el rey don Pedro. (III, xiii).

---

[8] The similarity of this scene to the one between Don Juan Tenorio and the comendador in *El Burlador de Sevilla* has caused

Too excited to sleep, Pedro calls together all of the courtiers of his palace and tells them of his resolution:

> El cielo ordena
> Que me acuerde del cielo.
> Obre la religión, renazca el cielo:
> Domingo soberano,
> Mucho por vos con Dios merezco y gano,
> Pues siendo Guzmán templo os ofrezco,
> Cuando ansí a los Guzmanes aborrezco. (III, xv). [9]

Preoccupied by the prophecy of the *sombra*, Pedro ponders
its awesome implications and realizes that there is still
hope that he may avert its fulfillment by an effort to regain
divine favor:

> Mas no me apercibiera
> Cuando decreto irrevocable fuera.
> Amenaza es de padre, si él lo dijo,
> Que nunca el padre ejecutó en el hijo. (III, xvii).

When Pedro reveals his intention to found a convent in
Madrid as evidence of his religious piety and repentance
for his sins, Alonso is amazed at the change in the king:
«Jamás he visto al Rey con tanto seso.» (III, xviii). Pedro orders that a stone statue of himself be placed in the
finished convent, and designates his daughter Juana as its
abbess. [10]

Doña Blanca de los Ríos and others to attribute this play to Tirso
de Molina.

[9] St. Dominic was a member of the same Guzmán family as
Leonor and her sons.

[10] In his *Historia de la villa y de la corte de Madrid* Amador de
los Ríos writes of a legend in which Pedro, having on a nocturnal
adventure supposedly killed a priest near the convent of Santo
Domingo, was pursued by the spirit of his victim each time that
he passed the scene of the violence. This legend, combined with
the fact the historical Pedro's many contributions to religious es-
tablishments, and the fact that his granddaughter Constanza was

Pedro states that he plans to build the convent on the very site where he had dropped his dagger during the interview with the *sombra*. When it is discovered that the dagger is missing, Pedro offers a rich reward to whomever finds it and returns it to him: «Tanto, que pondré a sus pies/ Mi vida y mi cetro Real.» (III, xviii). The irony of his overgenerous offer becomes clear to the astonished king when it is none other than his half-brother Enrique who returns this precious possession to him. Pedro grows even more suspicious of the Infante's ambition:

> Cuando a verme vienes, ¿vienes
> Con mi puñal en tu mano?
> O me amenazas tirano,
> O bárbaro me previenes:
> Ya me parece que tienes
> Imperio en mi fortaleza;
> Pues aspirando a la alteza
> Que en mis juventudes ves,
> Con el puñal a mis pies
> Amenazas mi cabeza. (III, xix).

Enrique insists upon his willingness to submit to the will of the king and his loyalty to his brother in so moving a manner that Pedro is convinced by his words, and seeks to embrace him in an expression of brotherly affection and forgiveness, but he shrinks from Enrique when he sees the dagger still in his hand he starts to draw his own sword in an instinctive reaction of self-defense. Immediately realizing his error, he admits that he has been unreasonably suspicious of his brother:

> Mi grandeza ha descompuesto
> Un aparente temor:
> El pecho tembló el rigor
> Dese puñal homicida. (III, xix).

---

abbess of this convent and had such a statue of her grandfather placed in the building, may have led to the mistaken impression that Pedro actually founded the convent.

Although Enrique insists upon his loyalty, Pedro is still fearful of the omen, since he realizes that it was God's will that Enrique find his dagger. Plagued by doubts in spite of his repentance of his sins and his new resolution to be an exemplary king, this King Pedro is either not so completely convinced of God's mercy as he has appeared to be, or he is unsure of his own ability to fulfil his resolution. The scene ends on a sinister note as Enrique protests his innocence of any treachery: «Ya verás que soy tu hermano.» And Pedro replies with a threat: «Ya verás que tu Rey soy.»

There is an obvious similarity between this scene between the half-brothers and the scene in *El médico de su honra*. In both Pedro feels threatened by the dagger which his brother is holding, and there is a foreboding of future violence in the momentary loss of self-control of the king, who actually shows evidence of a tendency to physical aggression toward his apparently innocent brother. In both plays King Pedro also makes a ironical statement of resolution to exercise his free will and attempt to avert the fulfillment of the omen by glorious deeds which will make him famous for his valor and his justice.

In the closing scenes of the play King Pedro appears enthroned and dressed in all of the regalia of his office. He calls to Enrique to stand near his throne in a sign of their reconciliation, and he bids his people enter to receive his justice: «Pues hoy quiero que celebre/ Mi justicia el mundo, donde/ En alabastro he de verme.» (III, xxi). Not content with the mere fulfillment of his duties to the best of his abilities, King Pedro reveals in this speech that what he really desires is eternal glory as the best and most exemplary *rey justiciero* in Castilian history. Just as he was jealous of his self-esteem as the most valiant swordsman in the land, so is he determined to be the most highly-esteemed monarch.

Reassured by his act of religious piety, Pedro feels more

secure in his position as king, and he is determined to disprove his reputation for cruelty by dispensing justice in his *audiencia*:

> Pueblo, yo soy vuestro Rey,
> Legítimo descendiente
> Del onceno rey Alfonso,
> Cuyo matrimonio fénix
> Aunque os dio tantos infantes,
> Un Rey os dio solamente.
> Yo soy: pedidme justicia. (III, xxii).

This speech reveals his extreme self-consciousness as he embarks upon this new phase of his kingship, and the fact that he finds it necessary to include a reference to the illegitimacy of his half-brothers indicates that he is still very much on the defensive.

Believing that the Infanzón has escaped, Pedro makes a show of severity when the people beg for clemency for Tello. He is dismayed to learn that the Infanzón and Cordero had been taken for horse thieves and taken into custody by the royal guard. Although Tello asks for clemency, Pedro feels compelled to remain firm in the resolution he had made to show no mercy toward him other than that which he had already granted as a friend: «No la alcanza quien no cree/ Los consejos del amigo,/ Y a un Rey justiciero vuelve.» (III, xxiii).

Pedro reviews Tello's crimes and asks Enrique if he does not believe them worthy of severe punishment. Enrique agrees, stating in an aside that he does so in order to appease his brother, but he later asks Pedro to pardon all three of the men in a demonstration of clemency which will be worthy of such an auspicious occasion. Pedro agrees to commend their loyalty to his brother, since it is by his efforts that they receive their freedom. Pedro asks Enrique to return his dagger, and as he leans to embrace his

brother the crown slips from his head. Enrique picks
it up from the floor and hands it to him.

His confidence shaken once again by this new omen,
Pedro says:

> ¡La corona y el puñal
> Juntas a tus manos vienen!
> No sé, hermano, qué imagine;
> No sé, Enrique, qué sospeche. (III, xxiii).

As the brothers embrace, Enrique utters the ironical and
ominous exclamation: «¡Quiera Dios/ Que esta amistad se
conserve!»

Throughout Act III the relationship between the brothers
has been marked by a contrast of the negative and suspicious attitude of King Pedro with the apparently affec-
tionate and cooperative attitude of Enrique, who defends his
brother against the criticism of his companion Mendoza and
even offers his own life as a pledge of loyalty to Pedro. It
is significant also that it is Enrique's positive action which
prevents the king from executing a severe death sentence
which is devoid of the very mercy which Pedro as a sinful
man hopes to receive from God, the Supreme Judge.

Enrique's lack of ambition and his total support of
Pedro are symbolized by his unhesitating return of the
dagger and the crown which seem to slip away from the
king's grasp of their own accord and gravitate toward him
as though by divine will. While Pedro is plagued by doubts
and is fearful of evil omens, Enrique is too optimistic to be
upset by repeated prophecies, and he remains cordial and
free of resentment in his dealings with his brother.

The four levels of authority and aggressiveness which
we observed in the first two acts now shift to include the
highest authority of all, as Rodrigo leaves the picture and
the *sombra* reveals to us the fact of his own limitations,
implicit in his suffering and his obedience to God, who

emerges as the originator of the three-stage confrontation which has finally brought about King Pedro's submission. Pedro, although outwardly confident and secure in his position, has suffered a psychological defeat at the hands of the *sombra* which may easily lead to his physical defeat at Montiel if he does not succeed in overcoming his apparently groundless fears and in moderating his violent passions.

The parallel between Pedro and Tello is complete in this act as Pedro is humbled into an admission of a power and authority higher than his own and he appeals for and receives the promise of divine mercy for his sins.

In *Los Ramírez de Arellano* we observe the physical defeat of King Pedro and the triumph of Enrique de Trastamara which would seem to be the natural outcome of the omens and prophecies of *El rey don Pedro en Madrid*. Lope makes it clear that the Castilian people favor Enrique and he insists upon the fact that it is God's will that the Conde become king. [11] Pedro appears only in Act III and is only a minor character in the drama. Lope might well have chosen not to have him appear on stage at all, since the scenes in which he appears do not further the action of the plot, which deals primarily with the actions and the characterization of another historical character of his reign, Juan Ramírez de Arellano.

Although his scenes are apparently unrelated interpolations in the main flow of the dramatic action, they are of unusual interest to us in our study of Lope's presentation of King Pedro, since they reveal his attitudes and preoccupations on the eve of his downfall. The picture of Pedro which Lope presents in these scenes is, if not by any means admirable, at least a sympathetic one. This Pedro is cognizant of his defeat and he reveals a helplessness and a gullibility which inspire pity in the reader. Stripped of his

----

[11] See Chapter II for a discussion of this aspect of the play.

power as king and exhausted from his struggles against his half-brother, Pedro becomes resigned to the fact that his only hope is to escape with his life, which will have little meaning because of the dishonor of his defeat.

We are prepared in a speech of Juan Ramírez in Act I for the hero's support of Enrique as the rightful King of Castilla: «La ley es lo principal,/ Luego el Rey.» (I, iii). In placing the Law before the King, Juan Ramírez is expressing the necessity for the observance of Natural Law by all men, including the king.   In Act III, out of dramatic necessity for presenting an opportunity for Juan Ramírez to state his reasons for joining the ranks of the bastard usurper, Lope has Pedro IV de Aragón, who in historical fact did not support Pedro in the Castilian civil wars, utter the following invective against Enrique:

> Enrique sólo alborota
> A España con sediciones
> Y ambición que el mundo nota,
> Pues con bastardos pendones
> Los vanos vientos azota.
> Créeme, que no será
> Rey de Castilla esta vez. (III, i).

Juan Ramírez counters this legitimist view of kingship with an indictment of Pedro as a rebel against the higher law of God, and he infers a divine sanction of Enrique:

> Sí hará; que enojado está
> Con su hermano aquel Juez
> Que el castigo y premio da.
> Y pues Pedro no se enmienda
> Ni quiere acortar la rienda
> A la crueldad y ambición,
> Dios dará la posesión
> A quien servirle pretenda. (III, i).

When Pedro de Aragón asks Juan Ramírez why Enrique has

not been more successful if it is God's will that he become king, he replies that man often cannot understand the workings of divine justice, and perhaps these trials are to assure the humility of Enrique.

After Juan Ramírez leaves, Pedro de Aragón talks with Pardo about the strife in Castilla and he hears that the entire kingdom is «quejosa de Pedro» and clamoring for Enrique to be king. The inference is that God's will is being carried out by the people, who have rallied to the support of Trastamara.

Enrique is allowed sufficient space to state his own case in the play, since he appears not only in Act III, which is the only one in which Pedro is presented, but he also has a long scene with Juan Ramírez in Act I. Enrique tells him that although he and his brothers are illegitimate, their nobility of birth, as blood relatives of the powerful Guzmán family, is as lofty as that of Pedro himself. He states that he was a loyal vassal of Pedro following the death of Alfonso XI: «Era justo que reinase;/ Yo lo obedezco y conozco.» (I, xviii). However, the widow and her sons were plagued by those jealous of their position and wealth and they were scorned by Pedro.

Enrique tells of the many offices assigned by Pedro to important nobles of the realm, ending with the bitter observation: «En fin, a todos/ Premiaron, y solamente/ Nos quitaron a nosotros.» [12] He insinuates that other acts of Pedro were of so nefarious a nature as not to be spoken of. He says that Pedro is unfit to be king, since he has lost the support of the people, who have turned to Enrique. He

---

[12] As we noted earlier, Enrique did not seek the throne in his own right until 1356, but he had been a traitor to Pedro almost from the outset of his reign. In constant rebellion against his half-brother, Enrique had previously supported the claims of Pedro de Portugal (1354) and was involved in insurrections in Asturias (1352) and Toledo (1355) before fleeing to Aragón and allying himself with Pedro IV.

hastens to add that he has not sought the office. The climax of this long speech and the reason given for his decision to seek the throne is the supposed order issued by Pedro to put Leonor de Guzmán to death. [13]

As Pedro enters the stage for the first time, he has just seen the priest who claims to be sent by Santo Domingo to warn him to either mend his ways or to face death at the hands of his brother Enrique. His opening speech reveals his anxiety and his supersitious dread of the omen: «¡Quitadmele de delante!/ ¡No le vean más mis ojos!» (III, xiii). [14] Lope does not mention the death of the priest. Besides shocking the sensibilities of his Catholic audience, [15] this would have detracted from the sympathetic picture of Pedro as a man which Lope is presenting.

Pedro complains petulantly of this supernatural reminder of his precarious situatión: «Todo para darme enojos,/ No siendo el mundo bastante.» He contemplates with horror the idea that «el cielo» may take vengeance upon him. As though fearful of the very name of God, he does not use the name «Dios» until late in the scene when he asserts himself to sally forth into battle against Enrique.

On the other hand, his companion, the Prince of Wales, [16]

[13] As we have already seen, this deed is ascribed by Ayala to María de Portugal. Lope's use of it is an anachronism, since Leonor died in 1351, in the second year of Pedro's reign, and the issue could hardly have been so fresh in 1356 as to have been Enrique's most compelling reason for wishing to dethrone Pedro.
[14] Ayala mentions the appearance of this priest in the ninth chapter of the eleventh year of his chronicle, saying that Pedro, although startled and dismayed by the prophecy, concluded that his enemies had induced the priest to come to him, and he had the priest burned to avenge the deception.
[15] Lope, a priest in later life, was a devout Catholic. His omission of any mention of the violent death of the priest in this play is noted by Menéndez y Pelayo, who believes it to be evidence of Lope's good taste and his sympathetic attitude toward King Pedro.
[16] Edward III of England and his son the Black Prince were supporting Pedro as the legitimate king against a bastard usurper.

speaks of God as the one who has made him King of Castilla and who, as Supreme Judge will decide which of the
two brothers will rule as his earthly representative. The
entire scene is permeated with dramatic irony. The en-
couraging words of the Prince of Wales would ring hollow in
the ears of the Golden Age audience, which knew the facts
of history.

In an attempt to convince Pedro to order his army into
action, the Prince says:

> Mueve el tuyo, gran señor,
> Y acábese de una vez
> Con el daño o el temor;
> Que Dios, que es sumo Juez,
> Dará a Castilla el mejor. (III, xiii).

The Prince of Wales accepts as proof of the rightness
of Pedro's claim the fact that he has thus far been victorious
against Enrique and must, therefore have God's favor. [17]
The audience knows that Enrique will be victorious over
Pedro, and this use of dramatic irony will give them the
impression of participating in divine justice. Reassured
by the words of his companion, Pedro suddenly recovers
from his fears and is impatient to meet and defeat his rivals: «¡Por Dios, que me he vuelto en mí/ lo que me habeis
advertido!/ ¡Muera Enrique! ¡Marcha, toca!»

Throughout this short scene the calm words of the Prince
of Wales are alternated with Pedro's impassioned exposition of the whole incident of the prophecy of the priest.
The details of the prophecy and the horror of the intended
victim, contrasting sharply with the Englishman's totally
confident and detached speeches, build to a climax of emotion when Pedro is suddenly moved to action and is eager

---

[17] Here we see an effective change in historical fact on the part
of Lope. Pedro was not victorious when he fled to Bordeaux to seek
the aid of the English.

to meet and kill the half-brother who is the source of his preoccupation.

In the short space of this scene the attitude of Pedro changes from one of inaction and insecurity to one of impatience and temerity. Pedro's hesitation is obviously not occasioned by a lack of courage but rather by his dread of the omen. Not until the very end of the scene does Pedro demonstrate his violent nature when he asserts himself for his last glorious attempt to regain his crown:

> ¡A Montiel!
> ¡Tanto el furor me provoca;
> Porque hasta verme con él
> Fuego arrojo por la boca (III, xiii).

As he is recovering his confidence, Pedro denounces angrily those who call him cruel: «Bueno es que el hacer justicia/ Llame Castilla crueldad.» The Prince of Wales agrees:

> Es la popular malicia:
> El vulgo desenfrenado,
> Al Rey justo llama airado,
> Y cruel al justiciero. (III, xiii).

Within its ironical context, this is a rather vain protestation. Lope reinforces the irony by having Pedro reply to these words which confirm his justice with the one words «¡Muera!» which has the force of an affirmation of the epithet «cruel».

Lope, who always had his audience in mind, made Pedro a sympathetic character as a man and a Spaniard in this scene by choosing the figure of the English prince for his companion. The Prince of Wales is presented as imposing and admirable if rather cold and impassive. In spite of his excellent qualities he would not be sympathetic to the Spanish audience because of his implacable attitude toward

the omens which were so great a part of the Spanish national drama: «Nunca han podido espantarme/ Falso agüero
o sueño vano.»

As the audience knew, the omen of Enrique's triumph is
anything but false. Pedro's anxiety is fully justified. This
fact could not fail to involve the Spanish onlooker and place
him in the position of mentally defending the anguished
Pedro against the scepticism of the foreigner. [18]

Lope changes the attitude of Pedro toward the priest
from that which is found in Ayala [19] by transferring to the
Prince of Wales the historical Pedro's suspicions that the
priest might have been sent by Enrique. This increases
further the psychological distance between the Spanish audience and the Black Prince when the latter says: «Y no
hay por que os alborote/ Que el que os dijo esa locura/
Fuese, señor, sacerdote.» A seventeenth-century Catholic
in Spain, the leader of the Counter-Reformation, would
mentally rally to the defense of his faith upon hearing such
words from the lips of an ancestor to future Protestants.

At the end of the play, as Pedro is fleeing the battle scene,
he curses his fate and wishes for an honorable death in battle rather than the dishonor of living on as a mere man: «¡Oh
suerte enemiga, atroz,/ Déjame morir primero/ Con acero
que con voces!» (III, xviii). Although he considers Enrique's victory a «maravilla,» the Prince of Wales tries to en-
courage Pedro: «Mal la fortuna conoces;/ Vive, que mudan-
za espero.» Up to this point, Lope has carefully created a
sympathetic and almost ideal picture of Enrique with a view
to enhancing the character of his supporter Juan Ramírez.
Having established the heroic statute of Juan Ramírez, Lope

---

[18] Enrique also concerns himself with omens in the scene
immediately following. He is dispensing his famous «mercedes,»
which he considers «bueno y dichoso agüero» that he will become
king.

[19] Ayala, *Crónica,* p. 507.

now balances the picture of the royal brothers' characters by exposing the darker side of the historical Trastamara.

When Mendo approaches Beltrán about allowing Pedro to escape, the Frenchman confers with Enrique, who says: «Dile que salga, Beltrán,/ Y que lo aceptas.» (III, xx). Beltrán agrees: «Yo voy;/ Que en tu pensamiento estoy.» Enrique then gathers together all of his supporters. Beltrán urges him on to the fratricide with the words: «Tu reino el cielo encamina:/ Vete y en mi tienda espera.» The interesting point here is that Lope would choose to show the details of the plot between Enrique and Beltrán, thus tarnishing the carefully-created image of Trastamara that he has been projecting throughout the play. This could easily have been avoided by merely making a passing mention of Pedro's death. The Golden Age audience already knew the story.

Why does Lope choose to dramatizc Enrique's treachery? In the opinion of this writer it is indicative of the fact that Lope sympathizes with Pedro as a man if he cannot condone the severity of his actions as king. In the interest of a balanced presentation of the brothers in this play he chooses to dramatize the entire episode of Pedro's downfall, leaving only the violence to take place off-stage.

Pedro is presented as the unsuspecting victim of this cruel plot between Enrique and the Frenchman. There is none of the anger or anxiety of his earlier speeches in his last trusting words to Beltrán as they leave the stage: «Ya vengo, francés gallardo... Fiarme en tus manos quiero» (III, xxi). The comforting words of the Frenchman heighten the horror of the audience's anticipation of the surprise awaiting Pedro: «Ven a mi tienda primero;/ Que todos son tus vasallos.»

The attitude of King Pedro as he goes meekly to his death is one of complete trust and non-aggression. Gone is the anger and vengefulness of the earlier scene with the Prince of Wales. Gone is the grandeur of the king of *El rey*

don Pedro en Madrid, who was conquered psychologically
by the *sombra,* but who remained defiant and suspicious of
his enemies in spite of his new resolution to be an exemplary and pious ruler.

We see now that this well-intentioned but all too human
king has not been able to regain the divine favor he was
in danger of losing in *El rey don Pedro en Madrid.* Still
a man of extremes, he did not learn to moderate his passions and rule with the self-possession and objectivity required of his position. His pride blinded him to his own
faults, and he must share the responsibility for his own
downfall.

CHAPTER VII

LOPE'S PEDRO I AND ALFONSO VIII: A COMPARISON OF TREATMENT

Lope de Vega, in addition to being the first poet to bring to the Spanish stage the unique personality of Pedro I, was also the first to dramatize two well-known legends: the pursuit of María Coronel by King Pedro, and the legendary love of Alfonso VIII for the Jewess of Toledo. In his plays *La corona merecida* and *Las paces de los reyes y judía de Toledo* [1] Lope attributed both of these legends to King Alfonso VIII de Castilla (1158-1214).

A close study of Lope's eight King Pedro plays in comparison with *La corona merecida* and *Las paces de los reyes,* in which he treats Alfonso VIII reveals the curious fact that Lope presented a far more sympathetic picture of King Pedro than of the noble Alfonso, a king for whom the poet had shown an admiration so great that he had even represented him on more than one occasion as a participant in the Third Crusade. Although he reveals aspects of Pedro's character in *Lo cierto por lo dudoso, La carbonera, El rey don Pedro en Madrid* and *Los Ramírez de Arellano* which

---

[1] See the edition of James A. Castañeda, *A Critical Edition of Lope de Vega's 'Las paces de los reyes y judía de Toledo'.* (University of North Carolina Press, 1962), and the edition of José F. Montesinos, *'La corona merecida' de Lope de Vega* (Centro de Estudios Hispánicos de Madrid, 1923).

demonstrate that he is not suited psychologically and emotionally to be king, Lope is consistently sympathetic to Pedro as a man.

In contrast to this sympathetic portrayal of Pedro is the picture of Alfonso VIII in *La corona merecida*, a play in which Lope chose to transfer to the latter monarch certain misdeeds belonging to the popular legends surrounding Pedro I. In both this play and in *Las paces de los reyes* Lope presents Alfonso as the willing victim of evil advice on the part of his counselors, who pander to his pleasures and aid him in his own dishonorable designs. On the other hand, Pedro I must bear the full responsibiliay for his errors, and we observe the traumatic effect of such guilt on the man in *El rey don Pedro en Madrid* and *Los Ramírez de Arellano*.

Whereas Alfonso makes serious errors which result in part from bad advice of his counselors, the errors of Pedro spring from his own passionate and vengeful nature, and are a manifestation of his excessive pride. Lope presents both Pedro and Alfonso as courageous in the face of the supernatural, and although both kings resolve to mend their ways and lead more exemplary lives, there is a sharp contrast between the suspicious nature and the insecurity of Pedro evident in all but two of Lope's King Pedro plays (*Audiencias* and *Ya anda la de Mazagatos*) and the confidence demonstrated by Alfonso.

Although he used a legend usually attributed to Pedro de Castilla in his *La corona merecida*, Lope made important changes which completely remove this play from the tradition of his King Pedro plays. He set the action in the time of Alfonso VIII rather than that of Pedro, he moved the locale from Sevilla to Burgos, and he changed the name of the heroine from María Coronel to Sol. [2] It is interesting

---

[2] López de Ayala records the fact that Pedro took as his mistress in 1358 María's sister Aldonza, but his attempted seduction of María belongs entirely to the realm of popular tradition.

to note that nowhere in this play does King Alfonso demonstrate the sentimentality or the love of the common people that we observed in Lope's King Pedro. Throughout
the dramatic action Alfonso concerns himself with nothing
more than the pursuit of his own selfish pleasures.

The honors which he gives and the justice which he dis-
penses are motivated by purely personal considerations, and
the picture of Alfonso as king which emerges from this play
is one of a tyrant who places himself above the law: «El
Rey es preferido a cualquier súbdito.» (III, vii). Unlike
Lope's King Pedro he places his faith in the advice of evil
counselors, and he seems to have no feelings of guilt for
his sin or pity for his victims: «Sólo el gusto del señor,/
Bien o mal, se ha de mirar.» (I, xi).

In Act III Alfonso admits that he has allowed his passion for the lady to cause him to appoint her husband to
the coveted position of *camarero mayor* when there were
other subjects more worthy of the honor, and he reveals
the extent of the faith which he has placed in his adviser
Pedro: «Eres mi amparo; no pares,/ Pues ves que ayuda
me das.» (III, i). A conversation between the two exposes
the selfishness of the king. Pedro sincerely regrets that the
husband of the heroine must die as a result of the plan he
has devised to aid the king. Alfonso replies coldly: «Deba-
jo de que todo va fundado/ En que viva tu Rey, ¿de qué te
afliges?» (III, vii). At the end of the play King Alfonso
admits his evil intentions and offers rewards to the offended parties. There is, however, no evidence that he has undergone any kind of conversion or that he has sincerely
repented of his sinful pursuit of the married lady.

In both of Lope's dramatic treatments of King Alfonso
we see the king in love, but the effect of this emotion on
his character is different in the plays. While in *La corona
merecida* he displays a brutal passion for another man's

wife, in *Las paces de los reyes* his love for Raquel [3] is one
of tender affection. According to legend, Alfonso VIII abandoned Queen Leonor de Inglaterra and disregarded the affairs of his realm for a period of some seven years while
enjoying the company of the Jewess.

In a conversation in *Las paces de los reyes* Alfonso tells
his good friend and adviser Garcerán of his difficult youth,
and reveals the fact that he was forced at an early age to
assume the role of a full-grown man in order to preserve
his kingdom. He expresses the realization that he has always been assured of God's favor: «El cielo me libró de tantos daños.» (II, iv). Although he appears to be content with
his present status, he expresses a need for activity: «Si no
ensancho a los reinos heredados,/ ¿Qué dejaré a mis hijos?»
(II, iv). Garcerán urges Alfonso to return to battle against
the Moors. Ironically, it is at this point that Alfonso spies
the lovely Jewess, who is bathing in the waters of the Tajo.

When his friend tries to warn him of the dangers of a
romantic involvement with her, Alfonso silences him with
a reminder of his own superior position as king: «Garcerán, el servir tiene dos caras:/ Verdad y gusto del señor.
Agora,/ Ponte en la de mi gusto.» (II, iv). Here Alfonso
makes a conscious choice not to listen to the voice of reason and caution but to allow his passions to dominate his
will. He also forces his friend Garcerán into the role of
an evil counselor. King Alfonso, never having had the opportunity to enjoy the frivolities of youth and the joys of

---

[3] As Castañeda shows in his study, it was Lope who, probably
inspired by the biblical story of Rachel, first gave the Jewess the
name Raquel in his epic poem *Jerusalén conquistada*, wherein he
shows Alfonso VIII as the companion of Richard the Lion-Hearted
on the Third Crusade, a rather capricious disregard for historical
fact which has earned him criticism, since there is no evidence
that Alfonso participated in the Crusade, and the city was not taken
by the Christians as the title suggests.

adolescent infatuation, is relatively inexperienced in the ways of love, and is taken completely by surprise when he begins to become aware of the dormant emotions within his own nature.

The King Alfonso of *Las paces de los reyes* is represented as a valiant and fearless soldier, but a man who allows his personal life to interfere with his duties as King of Castilla. Unlike King Pedro, he does not suffer from a sense of insecurity resulting from the constant threat of the loss of his throne to a rival, but he does exhibit a vengefulness similar to that of Pedro for a brief period following the death of Raquel, and before being brought to the realization of his sins by the visit of an angel. Like Lope's King Pedro, he is unafraid when faced with the supernatural. Having received a clearly-articulated divine warning, he also determines to exercise his will in order to regain the divine favor he has lost, but unlike the tormented Pedro, King Alfonso will be successful.

As we have seen, Lope's treatments of Pedro I and Alfonso VIII are similar in many respects. A product of the monarchical sentiment of his age, and a contributor to a literature rich in treatises on the desirable attributes and the education of a Christian prince, Lope naturally presents certain exemplary qualities in both monarchs. It is in the poet's revelation of the frailties of the mortal man behind the semi-divine facade that we begin to see the difference. Alfonso VIII enjoys the saintly reputation of a worthy Christian king ever active in the crusade against the enemies of medieval Spain. Since much of the blame for his errors may be placed upon the shoulders of his advisers, the legend of the Jewess of Toledo and the episode in *La corona merecida* merely add a more human quality without seriously detracting from his integrity as king. If it suited his dramatic purpose to present Alfonso as self-seeking and arbitrary in *La corona merecida*, Lope could be confident that this monarch would be redeemed by the fact of his unblemished historical image.

On the other hand, the character of Pedro I has been maligned to a greater or lesser degree in contemporary chronicles, ballads and popular traditions. His role as a conscientious *rey justiciero* is beclouded by a reputation for cruelty. In the face of such a potentially negative interpretation, and in an effort to present a balanced and sympathetic picture of this ambivalent monarch, Lope concentrated upon possible reasons for Pedro's actions, offering a more detailed exposition of this king's inner fears.

Although given to occasional episodes of self-indulgence, Lope's King Alfonso is cognizant of the demands of his role as King of Castilla and capable of the self-control necessary to fulfil it. [*] In contrast to this dramatic portrayal is the composite picture of Lope's King Pedro: a once self-possessed and prudent king who gradually loses his self-confidence and his control over his passions to the point where he is no longer fit to rule. Divested of his kingly aura and plagued by fear and suspicion, Pedro can no longer command respect, and he goes to his death a defeated and pitiable figure who, for all his shortcomings, cannot fail to elicit the reader's sympathy.

[*] See David H. Darst, «The Unity of *Las paces de los reyes y judía de Toledo*» in the Fall, 1971 issue of *Symposium* (XXV, 225-235).

CONCLUSION

The historical Pedro I de Castilla emerges as a rather antipathetic character in the contemporary chronicles and in the popular ballads which date from his reign. Popular tradition has tended to view him more sympathetically as a conscientious *rey justiciero* who was concerned with the defense of the common man against the tyranny of the powerful nobility and who had a sincere love for his people. The paradoxical historical image of Pedro as «el cruel» and «el justiciero» is a reflection of the turbulent century in which he lived, which was a period characterized by extremes of severe punishment and mercy in public justice.

Writing in the seventeenth century, Lope invests his medieval character with the aura of semi-divinity and the monarchical absolutism which were associated with the Divine Right of Kings, a concept totally alien to the unstable conditions of fourteenth-century Castilla.

Lope's treatment of King Pedro in these plays ranges from an idealized and completely apologetic picture of him in the *Audiencias del rey don Pedro* to the representation in *Los Ramírez de Arellano* of his having lost his right to rule because of past cruelty and his disregard for Natural Law. If one reads Lope's King Pedro plays in the order

suggested in this study one may detect a progressive change
in the character of Pedro. There is a steady loss of inner
security and self-confidence, an increasingly more suspicious
and less tolerant attitude, and a growing tendency to allow
his passion to influence his decisions.

A self-possessed, patient and prudent king in the *Audiencias del rey don Pedro*, King Pedro is presented as a well-meaning man who has been unjustly maligned because his
motives have been misunderstood. Unembittered by this
unfair reputation, and confident of his ability to rectify
the impression, Pedro endeavors to win the support of the
people by exemplary actions. As *rey justiciero*, he withholds judgment until he has heard all of the evidence, and
he demonstrates compassion even for those who are clearly
in error. At no time does he allow his own emotion to
influence his judgment.

In *Ya anda la de Mazagatos* Pedro is also patient,
compassionate and tolerant as a king, and self-confident and
unsuspicious as a man. He demonstrates that he sincerely
loves the common man, and he exhibits the personal courage
which is characteristic of all of the dramatic representations
of Pedro in Lope's drama.

In *El médico de su honra* King Pedro is an exemplary
rey justiciero and staunch defender of his subjects' honor.
Although he demonstrates concern about his reputation,
there is evidence both in this play and in *La niña de plata*
that he has a tendency to allow his emotions to influence
his judgment where his brother Enrique is involved. A
disappointment with him causes Pedro to begin to suspect
Enrique's motives, and this begins to undermine his self-confidence.

Pedro's distrust of Enrique which results from the latter's being a successful rival for a lady in *Lo cierto por lo
dudoso* is increased in *La carbonera* to the point where
Pedro is so suspicious of his brother's ambition and so

unsure of his own ability to maintain his position as king that he seeks to kill an innocent half-sister who might be of some aid to Enrique.

As Pedro's insecurity grows, he is guilty of more frequent incidents of rash and emotional behavior and his emotions and personal desires play a larger role in his decisions. He begins to use his hunting excursions as an escape from his duties, and he is increasingly more serious in his outlook as he begins to have very real doubts that he will be able to arrest the growth of popular support for Enrique to become king.

The fact that in *La carbonera* Pedro is unsuccessful in his attempts to offset his reputation for cruelty suggests that Lope viewed him as a man capable of cruelty who might bring upon himself his own downfall if he did not learn to control his passions and regain the objectivity necessary for the proper execution of his office as king.

In *El rey don Pedro en Madrid* Pedro is again confronted with his reputation for cruelty, a problem which is aiding the cause of his brother Enrique, who has aspirations to the Castilian throne. It is imperative that Pedro act in so exemplary a manner that he may by his own deeds demonstrate the injustice of the slander. In addition to this pressure, there is a divine warning to him in the guise of a *sombra* which admonishes him to repent of his sins and give concrete evidence of his humility before God or risk not only the loss of his throne but eternal damnation as well.

Pedro grows so suspicious of the apparently innocent Enrique that he observes him closely, anticipating a desire on his part to kill him. In his fear of his brother and in his dread of the omens and prophecies which abound in *El rey don Pedro en Madrid* Pedro demonstrates that he does not possess the peace of mind which will enable him to fulfil his solemn oath to mend his ways and be an exemplary king in order to regain divine favor and the support of his people.

We do not see King Pedro as a cruel and tyrannical king in any of the plays of Lope de Vega. In *Los Ramírez de Arellano* we hear of his cruel deeds, but when he appears on stage it is the defeated and broken man whom we see rather than the vengeful tyrant. He is a sympathetic character, for he is cognizant of his defeat, and he demonstrates a helplessness and a gullibility which inspire pity in the reader.

Lope is consistently sympathetic in his attitude toward Pedro as a man, although he demonstrates that he is not suited psychologically and emotionally to be king. In contrast to this sympathetic portrayal of Pedro is the picture of Alfonso VIII in *La corona merecida*, a play in which Lope chose to dramatize a legend closely associated with Pedro I, but attributing the actions to Alfonso VIII instead. In both this play and in *Las paces de los reyes* Lope presents Alfonso VIII as the victim of evil advice on the part of his counselors, who pander to his pleasures and aid him in his own dishonorable designs. On the other hand, Pedro I must bear the full responsibility for his errors. Lope presents both Pedro and Alfonso as courageous in the face of the supernatural, and although both kings resolve to mend their ways and lead more exemplary lives, there is a sharp contrast between the suspicious nature and the insecurity of Pedro and the confidence of Alfonso.

Whereas Alfonso is a king who as a man has made serious errors resulting in part from bad advice on the part of his counselors, the errors of Pedro spring from his own passionate and vengeful nature and are a manifestation of his excessive pride. It is this pride, which causes him to refuse to humble himself even before God until it is almost too late to save his own soul, which leads to his downfall as King of Castilla. Although well-meaning and courageous,

Pedro is too much a man of extremes to be able to maintain his position as king.

Thus, by an economical selection of his historical material, and use of the contemporary concepts of honor and Divine Right of Kings, Lope de Vega creates in his eight King Pedro plays a composite picture of this fourteenth-century king. Lope's Pedro undergoes a progressive development of character from total self-possession and prudence to a man who has lost his self-confidence and his control over his passions, a fact which renders him incapable of ruling Castilla and which results in the loss of his divine sanction as well as his life at the hands of Enrique de Trastamara.

Lope allows us to view intermittently the various stages of degeneration of Pedro I de Castilla from an unjustly slandered *rey justiciero* to a man divested of his kingly aura and plagued by fear and suspicion who comes to merit his epithet of «el cruel».

APPENDIX

APPENDIX

HISTORICAL PERSONS OF THE REIGN OF
PEDRO I DE CASTILLA

Abu Said, King Bermejo	Usurper of throne of Granada Ally of Pedro IV de Aragón
Juan Alfonso de Alburquerque	Illegitimate nephew of Alfonso IV de Portugal Principal minister of Pedro I de Castilla (1350-1353)
Alfonso	Only son of Pedro de Castilla and María de Padilla
Fernando de Aragón	Son of Leonor de Castilla and Alfonso IV de Aragón Successor to Castilian throne
Juan de Aragón	Brother of Fernando Married Isabel de Lara to become Señor de Vizcaya.
Pedro López de Ayala	Follower of Trastamara after 1366. Chronicler of reigns of Pedro I and Enrique II
Teresa de Ayala	Niece of the Chronicler Mistress of Pedro de Castilla Mother of María, Prioress of St. Dominic of Toledo, by Pedro de Castilla.
Beatriz	Eldest daughter of Pedro de Castilla and María de Padilla

Blanca de Borbón	Daughter of Duke of Borbón Married to Pedro de Castilla in 1353
Juan de Castilla	Son of Pedro de Castilla and Juana de Castro Father of Pedro and Constanza
Leonor de Castilla	Sister of Alfonso XI de Castilla Mother of Infantes Fernando and Juan
Pedro de Castilla	Son of Juan de Castilla by Elisa de Falces Archdeacon of Alarcón
Fernando de Castro	Loyal supporter of Pedro de Castilla Brother of Juana de Castro and half-brother of Inés and Alvar Pérez de Castro.
Alvar Pérez de Castro	Brother of Inés de Castro
Inés de Castro	Lady-in-waiting to Queen of Portugal, Constanza de Manuel Mistress of Pedro I de Portugal
Juana de Castro	Sister of Fernando de Castro, and half-sister of Inés and Alvar Pérez de Castro. Married to Pedro de Castilla in 1354
Juan de la Cerda	Husband of María Coronel Traitor to Pedro in 1357
Compañías Blancas	Marauding bands of adventurers who served as mercenary army Composed of men returning from the Crusades to find themselves «unemployed» who are joined by brigands and vagabonds Pope Innocent VI excommunicated them and they attacked Avignon in retaliation
Constanza	Second daughter of Pedro de Castilla and María de Padilla Wife of Duke of Lancaster
Constanza	Daughter of Juan de Castilla by Elisa de Falces Abbess of Santo Domingo el Real in Madrid

Aldonza Coronel	Wife of Alvar Pérez de Guzmán Mistress of Pedro de Castilla
María Coronel	Wife of Juan de la Cerda Founder and Abbess of Convent of Santa Inés in Sevilla
Cortés	Those of Castilla and León originated in the Councils of Toledo, composed of clergy and nobles King had exclusive right to summon, designate time and place and even composition of each session
Bertrand Du Guesclin	Beltrán Claquín, ally of Trastamara French leader of *Compañías Blancas*
Edward, the Black Prince	Prince of Wales, son of Edward III Ally of Pedro de Castilla
Enrique	Conde de Trastamara, later Enrique II, King of Castilla Son of Leonor de Guzmán and Alfonso XI de Castilla
Fadrique	Maestre de Santiago Brother and follower of brother Enrique de Trastamara
Alfonso Fernández Coronel	Traitor to Pedro at Aguilar in 1352 Father of María and Aldonza
Leonor de Guzmán	Mistress of Alfonso XI de Castilla Mother of Enrique, Fadrique, Tello and Sancho
Juan Fernández de Henestrosa	Uncle of María de Padilla Loyal supporter of Pedro de Castilla
María González de Henestrosa	Daughter of Juan Fernández de Henestrosa Mistress of Pedro de Castilla and mother of son Fernando
Isabel	Daughter of Pedro de Castilla and María de Padilla Married Edmund Langley, Earl of Cambridge and Duke of York
Isabel	Nurse of young Alfonso, son of Pedro I and María de Padilla Mistress of Pedro de Castilla and mother of Sancho and Diego

Samuel Leví	Jewish treasurer to Pedro de Castilla
Juana de Manuel	Daughter of Juan Manuel Wife of Enrique de Trastamara
Alvar Pérez de Guzmán	Traitor to Pedro de Castilla in 1357 Husband of Aldonza Coronel
María de Portugal	Wife of Alfonso XI de Castilla Sister of Alfonso IV de Portugal Mother of Pedro I de Castilla
Mohammed V	King of Granada and ally of Pedro de Castilla
Juan Núñez de Lara	Grandson of Fernando de la Cerda and great-grandson of Alfonso X de Castilla Successor to Castilian throne
Urraca Osorio	Mother of Juan Alfonso de Guzmán, who was a traitor to Pedro She was publically executed in Sevilla after her son's escape
Juan Núñez de Prado	Maestre de Calatrava, killed by Diego García de Padilla
Diego García de Padilla	Brother of María de Padilla Maestre de Calatrava
María de Padilla	Daughter of Juan García de Padilla Mistress of Pedro I de Castilla Mother of Alfonso, Beatriz, Constanza and Inés
Francisco de Perellós	Conde de Rueda, an ally of Pedro IV de Aragón
Juan Ramírez de Arellano	Navarrese nobleman, an ally of Enrique de Trastamara
Mendo Rodríguez de Sanabria	Loyal supporter of Pedro I de Castilla
Sancho	Brother of Enrique de Trastamara Later Conde de Alburquerque Married Beatriz daughter of Pedro I de Portugal and Inés de Castro
Tello	Brother of Trastamara Husband of Juana de Lara, and threby claiming to be Señor de Vizcaya

Rebellion and ...

1350

Alfonso XI dies of plague at Gibraltar March 23. Pedro I King of
Castilla
Leonor de Guzmán taken into custody at Sevilla
Enrique visits mother, who arranges secret consummation of his
marriage to Juana de Manuel May 17
Enrique flees from Sevilla
Serious illness of young king polarizes nobles in support of rival
successors to throne Fernando de Aragón and Juan Núñez de
Lara
Pedro recovers and spends rest of year in Andalucía

1351

Fadrique visits mother in Llerena before she is moved to Talavera
and put to death by order of María de Portugal
Juan Núñez de Lara dies and Pedro seizes his lands and takes sis-
ters Juana and Isabel into custody
Death of Garcilaso de la Vega in Burgos by order of Alburquerque
Cortes of Valladolid
Negotiations between Castilla, Pope Clement VI and John II of
France for marriage between Pedro and Blanca de Borbón

1352

Rebellion and subsequent death of Alfonso Fernández Coronel at
  Aguilar
Rebellion and later reconciliation of Enrique de Trastamara in As-
  turias
Pedro meets María de Padilla

1353

Birth of Beatriz to Pedro and María de Padilla
Wedding of Pedro to Blanca de Borbón in Valladolid June 3
Two days later he abandons bride to return to María de Padilla in
  nearby Montalván
Alburquerque steadily losing power as Padilla family rises
Blanca is sent to Arévalo
María de Padilla receives papal permission to found Convent of
  Santa Clara in Astudillo

1354

Tello marries Juana de Lara to become Señor de Vizcaya
Fadrique and Enrique, newly reconciled with Pedro, are named
  adelantados of the Portuguese frontier, whereupon they, with
  with their former rival Alburquerque, form a cabal against Pedro
  in support of the claims of Pedro de Portugal to the throne of
  Castilla
Diego García de Padilla is made Maestre de Calatrava and he has
  the former Maestre, Juan Núñez de Prado, executed
Pedro marries Juana de Castro at Cuéllar
Pedro returns to María de Padilla after one day
Pedro arranges for Juan de Aragón to marry Isabel de Lara and
  take the title of Señor de Vizcaya
Birth of Constanza to Pedro and María de Padilla
Blanca is moved to Toledo, which rises up in revolt in support of
  her claim as queen
Infantes of Aragón join with Alburquerque aginst Pedro along with
  María de Portugal and Leonor de Castilla
Innocent VI excommunicates Pedro
Death of Alburquerque
Vistas of Tejadillo
Pedro taken prisoner at Toro
One month later he escapes and goes to Segovia

1355

Cortes in Burgos
Inés de Castro dies at Coimbra January 7
Enrique enters Toledo and massacres Jews
Pedro arrives in Toledo and retakes city
Blanca is moved to Sigüenza
Birth of Isabel to Pedro and María de Padilla

1356

Pedro takes Toro and severely punishes rebel nobles
Queen mother María returns to Portugal
Enrique flees to France
Pedro is reconciled with Fadrique
Beginning of war with Aragón

1357

Agreement between Pedro IV de Aragón and Enrique against Pedro
    de Castilla January 20
Juan de la Cerda and Alvar Pérez de Guzmán join Aragón
Alvar Pérez de Guzmán escapes, but Juan de la Cerda is taken
    prisoner and executed in Sevilla
Treaty between Castilla and Aragón is negotiated by papal legate
    Cardinal Guillén
Death of Alonso IV de Portugal

1358

Pedro takes Aldonza Coronel as mistress
Juana escapes custody to join husband Enrique
Fernando de Aragón joins Aragón
Death of Fadrique in Alcázar de Sevilla by order of Pedro May 29
Tello flees from Vizcaya to Bayona
Death of Juan de Aragón in Bilbao by order of Pedro
Renewal of war with Aragón
Castilian fleet is destroyed in storm

1359

Papal legate Cardinal Boloña comes to Castilla to try to arrange
    peace terms with Aragón

Pedro orders death of Leonor de Castilla
Blanca is sent to Xérez de la Frontera
Pedro accompanies fleet to Barcelona
Son Alfonso born to Pedro and María de Padilla
Juan Fernández de Henestrosa dies in Battle of Araviana
Death of youngest bastard brothers Juan and Pedro at Carmona
   by order of Pedro

1360

Pedro orders death of Gutier Fernández de Toledo
Ghostly apparition of Dominican priest
Pedro returns to Sevilla
Samuel Leví is seized
Exchange of prisoners with Pedro of Portugal
Pedro de Portugal declares Inés de Castro queen

1361

Abu Said, King Bermejo, usurps throne of King Mohammed V of
   Granada, ally of Pedro
In face of possible alliance of Granada and Aragón Pedro signs peace
   treaty with Aragón May 13
Enrique goes to France
Death of Blanca de Borbón
Death of María de Padilla

1362

Diego García de Padilla captured, then released by King Bermejo
Pedro has King Bermejo killed for his treachery in negotiating
   with Aragón
At *Cortes* of Sevilla Pedro declares María de Padilla legitimate
   queen
Enrique and *Compañías Blancas* join with Pedro IV de Aragón to
   renew war with Castilla
Pedro negotiates alliance with Carlos II de Navarra
Pedro takes Calatayud
Pedro registers will at Sevilla November 18
Death of Alfonso, only son of Pedro and María de Padilla

1363

Pedro negotiates alliance with England and Edward, Prince of Wales

At *Cortés* of Bubierca Pedro names daughters heirs to throne of Castilla

Pedro IV de Aragón orders death of his brother Fernando at Castellón July 20.

Pact between Carlos de Navarra and Pedro IV

Pact of Monzón between Pedro IV and Trastamara March 31

Pact of Murviedro between Castilla and Aragón

Meeting at Castle of Sos between Pedro IV and Carlos II

Meeting at Castle of Uncastillo between Pedro IV, Carlos II and Trastamara August 25

1364

Pedro IV de Aragón orders death of minister Bernardo de Cabrera

Pact at Sos between Carlos II, Pedro IV and Trastamara against Pedro de Castilla March 1

Aragonese enter Valencia

Tello aids Pedro against Enrique

Pedro is saved from shipwreck in storm and makes pilgrimage to give thanks

1365

Pedro de Castilla takes Orihuela June 7

Death of Alonso de Guzmán by order of Pedro

Pedro IV de Aragón takes Murviedro

Enrique, Pope Urban V and the Kings of France and Aragón come to agreement with Bertrand Du Guesclin and the *Compañías Blancas* to invade Castilla

1366

Enrique crosses into Castilla and is proclaimed King at Calahorra March 16

When he hears that Enrique has entered Toledo, Pedro goes to Portugal and thence to Bordeaux to seal pact with Edward, the Black Prince and Carlos II de Navarra

On his way through Galicia, Pedro orders the death of the Arch-
    bishop of Santiago for treachery in supporting Enrique
Enrique and Bertrand Du Guesclin take Burgos, Toledo and Sevilla
Enrique holds *Cortes* in Burgos and declares his son Juan heir to
    throne of Castilla
Carlos II de Navarra meets with Trastamara
Carlos II pretends to be held captive at Castle of Borja to escape
    conflicting alliances

1367

Death of Pedro I de Portugal January 18
Pedro de Castilla victorious at Battle of Nájera April 13
Enrique escapes and flees to France
Treaty between Castilla and Aragón August 13
Pedro orders death of Urraca Osorio in Sevilla
Black Prince becomes ill and leaves Spain
Enrique makes new alliance with France
Enrique enters first Calahorra then Burgos
Córdoba, Jaén, Palencia, Valladolid, Avila, Salamanca and Segovia
    declare for Enrique

1368

Tello allies self with Carlos II de Navarra
Enrique takes Dueñas, León and Madrid and lays siege to Toledo
    April 30
Pedro's forces are relatively inactive
Pedro takes sons Sancho and Diego to Carmona

1369

Pedro goes to aid of Toledo, and on the way from Sevilla he meets
    Enrique at Montiel
Treachery of Diego García de Padilla
Montiel battle lost, Pedro takes refuge in Castle
Death of Pedro I de Castilla March 23

BIBLIOGRAPHY

BIBLIOGRAPHY

BOOKS

Altamira y Crevea, Rafael. *Historia de España y de la civilización española*. II. Madrid: J. Gili, 1929.

Amador de los Ríos, José. *Historia de la villa y de la corte de Madrid*. I. Madrid, 1860.

Amador de los Ríos, Rodrigo. *La leyenda del rey Bermejo*. Barcelona: Biblioteca «Arte y Letras,» 1890.

Arco y Garay, Ricardo del. *La sociedad española en las obras de Lope de Vega*. Madrid: Escelicer, 1941.

Atkinson, William C. *A History of Spain and Portugal*. London: Penguin Books, 1960.

Ballesteros y Beretta, Antonio. *Historia de España y su influencia en la historia universal*. III. 2nd ed. Barcelona: Salvat, 1948.

Beneyto Pérez, Juan. *Textos políticos de la baja edad media*. Madrid: Instituto de Estudios Políticos, 1944.

Brown, Robert B. *Bibliografía de las comedias históricas, tradicionales y legendarias de Lope de Vega*. State University of Iowa Studies in Spanish Language and Literature, X. Mexico City: Editorial Academia, 1958.

Carlyle, Robert S., and A. J. Carlyle. *A History of Medieval Political Theory in the West*. Irregular editions. 6 vols. Edinburgh and London: Blackwood and Sons, 1930-1938.

Casa, Frank P. *The Dramatic Craftsmanship of Moreto*. Cambridge, Massachusetts: Harvard University Press, 1966.

Castañeda, James A. *A Critical Edition of Lope de Vega's Las paces de los reyes y judía de Toledo*. Studies in Romance Languages and Literature, XL. Chapel Hill: University of North Carolina Press, 1962.

Catalina García, Juan. *Castilla y León durante los reinados de Pedro I, Enrique II, Juan I y Enrique III.* Vol. III of *Historia General de España.* Edited by Antonio Cánovas del Castillo. 20 vols. Madrid: Real Academia de la Historia, 1893.

Catálogo de la exposición bibliográfico de Lope de Vega, organizada por la Biblioteca Nacional. Madrid: Junta del Centenario de Lope de Vega, 1935.

Chapman, Carles E. *A History of Spain.* New York: The Free Press, 1965.

Cotarelo y Mori, Emilio. *Tirso: investigaciones biobibliográficas.* Madrid: Enrique Rubiños, 1893.

Diccionario de la lengua española. Madrid: Real Academia Española, 1970.

Diez de Games, Gutierre. *El Victorial: Crónica de Don Pedro Niño, Conde de Buelna.* Madrid: Espasa-Calpe, 1940.

Dillon, John Talbort. *The History of the Reign of Peter the Cruel, The King of Castile and León.* London: 1788.

Escritores en prosa anteriores al siglo XV. Biblioteca de autores españoles. Edited by Pascual de Gayangos. LI. Madrid: Sucesores de Hernando, 1922.

Ferrer del Río, Antonio. *Examen histórico-crítico del reinado de don Pedro de Castilla.* Madrid: Real Academia Española, 1863.

Figgis, John Neville. *The Divine Right of Kings.* New York: Harper and Row, 1965.

Floranes, Rafael de. *Vida literaria del Canciller Mayor de Castilla D. Pedro López de Ayala.* Colección de documentos inéditos para la historia de España. XIX. Madrid: Viuda de Calero, 1852.

Fuensanta del Valle, el Marqués de, ed. *Cuarta Crónica General.* Colección de documentos inéditos para la historia de España. CVI. Madrid, 1893.

Froissart, Jean. *Chroniques 1322-1378. Oeuvres de Froissart.* Edited by Kervyn de Lettenhove. XVII. Reprint. Osnabrück: Biblio Verlag, 1967.

Grismer, Raymond L. *Bibliography of Lope de Vega.* 2 vols. Minneapolis: Burgess-Beckwith, 1965.

Hamilton, Bernice. *Political Thought in Sixteenth-Century Spain: A Study of the Political Ideas of Victoria, De Soto, Suárez and Molina.* London: Oxford University Press, 1963.

Hartzenbusch, Juan Eugenio, ed. *Comedias escogidas de Fray Gabriel Téllez.* Biblioteca de autores españoles. V. Madrid: Hernando, 1930.

— *Comedias escogidas de Lope de Vega.* Biblioteca de autores españoles. XXIV, XLI. Madrid: Hernando, 1925.

Huizinga, Johan. *The Waning of the Middle Ages.* London: Edward and Co., 1924.

Jiménez de Rada, Rodrigo. *La Crónica de España.* Colección de documentos inéditos para la historia de España. CVI. Reprint. Madrid: Real Academia de la Historia, 1966.

Jones, C. A., ed. *El médico de su honra of Calderón de la Barca.* Oxford: The Clarendon Press, 1961.

Kantorowicz, Ernst H. *The King's Two Bodies: A Study in Mediaeval Political Theology.* Princeton: University Press, 1957.

Kern, Fritz, *Kingship and Law in the Middle Ages.* Studies in Mediaeval History. Oxford: Basil Blackwell, 1939.

La Barrera y Leirado, Alberto Cayetano de. *Catálogo bibliográfico del teatro antiguo español desde sus orígenes hasta mediados del siglo XVIII.* Madrid: Rivadeneyra, 1860.

Lewy, Guenter. *Constitutionalism and Statecraft During the Golden Age of Spain: A Study of the Political Philosophy of Juan de Mariana, S. J.* Travaux D'Humanisme et Renaissance. XXXVI. Geneva: Librairie E. Droz, 1960.

Livermore, Harold. *A History of Spain.* London: George Allen and Unwin, Ltd., 1958.

López de Ayala, Pedro. *Crónica de don Pedro Primero.* Biblioteca de autores españoles. LXVI. Madrid: Rivadeneyra, 1953.

— *Rimado de palacio.* Biblioteca de autores españoles. LVII. Madrid: Hernando, 1925, 424-476.

McClelland, Ivy L. *Tirso de Molina: Studies in Dramatic Realism.* Liverpool: Studies in Spanish Literature, Third Series. Institute of Hispanic Studies, 1948.

McCready, Warren Thomas. *Bibliografía temática de estudios sobre el teatro español antiguo.* Toronto: University Press, 1966.

Madden, Marie. *Political Theory and Law in Medieval Spain.* New York: Fordham University Press, 1930.

Maravall, José Antonio. *El concepto de España en la Edad Media.* Madrid: Instituto de Estudios Políticos, 1954 .

Mariana, Juan de. *Del rey y de la institución real. Obras.* Biblioteca de autores españoles. XXI. Madrid: Hernando, 1909, 463-576.

— *Historia de España.* Biblioteca de autores españoles. XXX. Madrid: Hernando, 1931.

Menéndez y Pelayo, Marcelino. *Antología de poetas líricos castellanos.* XXIII. Santander: Consejo Superior de Investigaciones Científicas, 1944.

— *Estudios sobre Lope de Vega.* 6 vols. *Obras Completas.* Madrid: Consejo Superior de Investigaciones Científicas, 1949.

Meregalli, Franco. *Pietro de Castiglia nella Letteratura.* Milano: La Golliardica, 1951.

Mérimée, Prosper. *Histoire de Don Pèdre Ier Roi de Castille.* París: Charpentier, 1865.

Montesinos, José F. *Estudios sobre Lope de Vega.* México, D. F.: Editorial Galatea, 1951.

— ed. *La corona merecida de Lope de Vega.* Teatro antiguo español. V. Madrid: Centro de Estudios Hispánicos, 1923.

Moore, Jerome Aaron. *The Romancero in the Chronicle-Legend Plays of Lope de Vega.* Philadelphia: University of Pennsylvania Press, 1940.

Montoto, José María. *Historia del reinado de D. Pedro de Castilla, llamado el Cruel.* Seville, 1847.

Morley, Sylvanus, and Courtney Bruerton. *The Chronology of Lope de Vega's Comedias with a Discussion of Doubtful Attributions.* New York: Modern Language Association, 1940.

Muñoz Peña, Pedro. *El teatro de Tirso de Molina.* Valladolid, 1889.

Ortiz de Zúñiga, Diego. *Anales eclesiásticos y seculares de la ciudad de Sevilla.* II. Madrid: Imprenta Real, 1795.

Parker, Jack Horace and Arthur M. Fox. *Lope de Vega Studies: 1937-1962: A Critical Survey and Annotated Bibliography.* Toronto: University Press, 1964.

Pemán, José María. *Algunos valores fundamentales del teatro de Lope de Vega.* Buenos Aires: Cumbre, 1942.

Pérez Gómez, Antonio, ed. *Romancero del Rey Don Pedro.* Valencia: ... la fonte que mana y corre ..., 1954.

Pfandl, Ludwig. *Cultura y costumbres del pueblo español de los siglos XVI y XVII.* Barcelona: Editorial Araluce, 1959.

Pietri, François. *Pierre le Cruel: Le vrai et le faux.* París, 1961.

Primera crónica general. Edited by Ramón Menéndez Pidal. Nueva Biblioteca de autores españoles. V. Madrid: Bailly-Baillière, 1906.

Ramírez de Arellano, Diana. *Los Ramírez de Arellano de Lope de Vega: Contribución al estudio de las comedias genealógicas de Lope de Vega.* Madrid: Consejo Superior de Investigaciones Científicas, 1954.

Rennert, Hugo Albert. *The Life of Lope de Vega (1562-1635).* Glasgow: Cowans and Gray, University Press, 1904.

— *The Spanish Stage in the Time of Lope de Vega.* Reprint. New York: Dover Publications, 1963.

— and Américo Castro. *Vida de Lope de Vega.* Madrid: Sucesores de Hernando, 1919.

Ríos, Blanca de los. *Tirso de Molina: Obras Completas.* III. Madrid: Aguilar, 1958.

Sánchez Arjona, José. *Noticias referentes a los anales del teatro en Sevilla.* Seville, 1891.

Sitges, J. B. *Las mujeres del rey don Pedro I de Castilla.* Madrid: Sucesores de Rivadeneyra, 1910.

Sloman, Albert E. *The Dramatic Craftsmanship of Calderón.* Oxford: The Dolphin Book Co., 1958.

Storer, Edmund. *Peter the Cruel.* London: John Lane Co., 1911.

Ticknor, George. *A History of Spanish Literature.* II. 6th Am. ed. New York: Gordian Press, 1965.

Underhill, John Garret, ed. *Four Plays by Lope de Vega.* New York: C. Scribner's Sons, 1936.

Vega Carpio, Lope Félix de. *Obras.* 13 vols. Edited by Emilio Cotarelo y Mori, *et al.* Madrid: Real Academia Española, 1916-1930.

— *Obras.* 15 vols. Edited by Marcelino Menéndez y Pelayo. Madrid: Real Academia Española, 1890-1913.

Vossler, Karl. *Lope de Vega y su tiempo*. Translated by Ramón de la Serna. Madrid: Revista de Occidente, 1933.

ARTICLES

Arjona, Jaime Homero. «Ten Plays Attributed to Lope de Vega.» *Hispanic Review*, XXXVII (October, 1960), 319-340.

Bataillon, Marcel. «La nouvelle chronologie de la comedia lopesque: de la metrique a l'histoire,» *Bulletin Hispanique*, XLVII (1946), 227-237.

Bersas, H. N. «Lope de Vega and the Post of Royal Chronicler,» *Hispanic Review*, XXI (April, 1963), 109-117.

Born, Lester Kruger. «The Perfect Prince: A Study in Thirteenth- and Fourteenth-Century Ideals,» *Speculum*, III (1928), 470-504.

Buchanan, Milton. «The Chronology of Lope de Vega's Plays,» *University of Toronto Studies, Philological Series*, VI (1920), 3-25.

Cánovas y Vallejo, José. «*El médico de su honra, estudio crítico,*» *Ilustración Española y Americana de Madrid*, XLIX (1905), 290-294, 314-315.

Catalán Menéndez Pidal, Diego. «'Nunca viera jaboneros tan bien vender su jabón,' Romance histórico del rey don Pedro, del año 1357,» *Boletín de la Real Academia Española*, XXXII (mayo-agosto, 1952), 233-245.

— «Un romance histórico de Alfonso XI,» *Estudios dedicados a Menéndez Pidal*, VI. Madrid: Consejo Superior de Investigaciones Científicos, 1956, 259-285.

Cirot, Georges. «Le témoignage de López de Ayala au sujet de D. Fadrique, frère de Pierre-le-Cruel.» *Hispania*, V (París: janvier-décembre, 1922), 70-76.

Davis, Gifford. «The Incipient Sentiment of Nationality in Medieval Castile: *The Patrimonio Real*,» *Speculum*, XII (1937), 351-358.

Durán, Manuel. «Lope de Vega y el teatro de acción,» *Hispanófila*, VI (1963), 3-14.

Entwistle, William J. «The *Romancero del rey Don Pedro* in Ayala and the *Cuarta Crónica General*,» *Modern Language Review*, XXV (1930), 306-326.

Gardiner, N. E. «The Ballads of the Prior de San Juan,» *Modern Language Review*, XXXIV (October, 1939), 550-556.

Gratia Dei, Pedro de. «Historia del rey don Pedro y su descendencia que es el linaje de los Castillas,» *Semanario erudito*, XXVIII (Madrid; Valladares, 1788), 224-268.

Heaton, H. C. «Lope de Vega's *Parte XXVIII Extravagante*,» *Romanic Review*, XV (1924), 100-104.

— «On the Text of Lope de Vega's *El médico de su honra*,» *Todd Memorial Volumes*, I. New York: Books for Libraries Press, 1968, 201-209.

Herrero-García, Miguel. «Ideología española del siglo XVII: La nobleza,» *Revista de Filología Española*, XIV (1927), 33-58, 161-175.
— «La monarquía teorética de Lope de Vega,» *Fénix*, No. 2 (April 27,
1935), 179-224.
— «La monarquía teorética de Lope de Vega,» *Fénix*, No. 3 (June,
1935), 305-362.
Hesse, Everett W. «La concepción calderoniana del príncipe perfecto
en *La vida es sueño*,» *Clavileño*, IV (1953), 4-12.
Huarte, Amalio. «Sobre la comedia *El Infanzón de Illescas de Lope
de Vega*,» *Boletín de la Biblioteca Menéndez y Pelayo*, XVI (abril-
junio, 1934), 97-126.
Kennedy, Ruth Lee. «*La prudencia en la mujer* and the Ambient
that Brought it Forth,» *PMLA*, LXIII (1948), 1131-1190.
Kossoff, A. David. «*El médico de su honra* and 'La amiga de Bernal
Francés,'» *Hispanic Review*, XXIV (1956), 66-70.
Lomba y Pedraja, José R. «El Rey don Pedro en el teatro,» *Homena-
je a Menéndez y Pelayo*. II. Madrid, 1899, 257-339.
Machado, Manuel: «*La niña de plata* refundida por Cañizares,» *Re-
vista de Archivos, Bibliotecas y Museos*, I (1924), 36-45.
Menéndez y Pelayo, Marcelino. «Revista Crítica,» *La España Moder-
na*, VI (April 1894), 117-157.
Merriman, Roger Bigelow. «The *Cortes* of the Spanish Kindoms in
the Later Middle Ages,» *American Historical Review*, XVI (April,
1911), 476-495.
Montesinos, José F. «Contribución al estudio del teatro de Lope de
Vega,» *Revista de Filología Española*, VIII (1921), 131-140.
Montoto, Santiago, «Lope de Vega y la Nobleza,» *Boletín de la Real
Academia Española*, XXII (1935), 657-665.
Morley, S. Griswold. «Notes on the Bibliography of Lope de Vega's
Comedias,» *Modern Philology*, XX (1922-1923), 201-277.
— «Lope de Vega's *Peregrino Lists*,» *University of California Publi-
cations in Modern Philology*, XXXIII. Berkeley: University Press,
1930, 345-366.
— «Lope de Vega's *Peregrino* Lists Not *Termini a quo*,» *Modern
Language Notes*, XLIX (1934), 11-12.
— «*Ya anda la de Mazagatos*. Comedia desconocida atribuida a Lope
de Vega,» *Bulletin Hispanique*, XXV (1923), 212-225.
— «*Ya anda la de Mazagatos*. Comedia desconocida atribuida a
Lope de Vega,» *Bulletin Hispanique*, XXVI (1924), 97-191.
— And Courtney Bruerton. «Addenda to the Chronology of Lope de
Vega's *Comedias*,» *Hispanic Review*, XV (1947), 50-71.
Parker, Alexander A. «The Approach to the Spanish Drama of the
Golden Age,» *Tulane Drama Review*, IV (September, 1959), 42-59.
Pemartín, José. «La idea monárquica de Lope de Vega,» *Acción Es-
pañola de Madrid*, XIV (1935), 417-450.
Reid, John T. «St. John's Day in Spanish Literature,» *Hispania*,
XVIII (1935), 401-412.
Rennert, Hugo A. «Bibliography of the Dramatic Works of Lope

de Vega Based Upon the Catalogue of John Rutter Chorley,»
Revue Hispanique, XXXIII (1915), 1-284.
— «*La niña de plata*,» *Modern Language Review*, I (1906), 107-108.
Ríos y Ríos, Angel de los «Cómo y por qué se llamó a D. Pedro el
Cruel, Pero Gil,» *Boletín de la Real Academia de la Historia*,
XXXVI (1900), 61-5.
Sears, Helen L. «The *Rimado de Palacio* and the 'De Regimine Prin-
cipum' Tradition of the Middle Ages,» *Hispanic Review*, XX (Ja-
nuary, 1952), 1-27.
Sloman, Albert E. «Calderón's *El médico de su honra* and *La amiga
de Bernal Francés*,» *Bulletin of Hispanic Studies*, XXXIV (1957),
168-169.
Torres y Franco Romero, Lucas de. «Las bodas del Rey D. Pedro
de Castilla,» *Revista de Archivos, Bibliotecas y Museos*, XX (1909),
28-42, 247-262.
Valbuena Briones, Angel. «Simbolismo: La caída del caballo,» *Perspectiva crítica de los dramas de Calderón*. Madrid. Ediciones
Rialp, 1965, 35-53.
Watson, A. Irvine. «Peter the Just or Peter the Cruel,» *Romanistisches Jahrbuch*, XIV (1963), 322-346.
Wilson, E. M. «Gerald Brenan's Calderón,» *Boletín de los Comediantes*, IV (Spring, 1952), 6-8.
— «Las discreción de don Lope de Almeida,» *Clavileño* (mayo-junio,
1951), 1-10.

UNPUBLISHED MATERIAL

Asturias, Sister Mary Rosario. «Critical Edition of *El rey don Pedro
en Madrid*.» Unpublished doctoral dissertation, University of
Southern California, 1964.
Brown, Sandra Lou. «Tirso de Molina His Treatment of Medieval
Spanish History.» Unpublished doctoral dissertation, University
of North Carolina at Chapel Hill, 1969.
Coleman, Sarah Embry. «Cuaderno otorgado a los procuradores en
las *Cortes* de Valladolid de 1351.» Unpublished doctoral dissertation, Department of Romance Languages and Literature, Univer-
sity of Chicago, 1939.
Fox, Mary Florence. «Spanish Ballad Treatment of Don Pedro el
Cruel.» Unpublished Master's thesis, University of Illinois, 1946.
Manson, William R. «Attitudes Toward Authority as Expressed in Typical Spanish Plays of the Golden Age.» Unpublished doctoral dissertation, University of North Carolina at Chapel Hill, 1963.
Rovner, Philip. «Lope de Vega on Kingship.» Unpublished doctoral
dissertation, University of Maryland, 1958.
Schons, Emily. «New Material on the Dramatic Treatment of Peter
the Cruel of Castile and the Diffusion of the Legend in France,

Germany and England.» Unpublished doctoral dissertation, University of Chicago, 1933.

Schuster, Edward J. «Yo, el Rey: A Study of the Development of Monarchical Absolutism in the Spanish Golden Age and Its Influence on the Literature of the Period.» Unpublished doctoral dissertation, University of Minnesota, 1950.

Seymour, Consuelo Willard. «Popular Elments and the Idea of Justice in the *Comedias* of Lope de Vega.» Unpublished doctoral dissertation, Stanford University, 1953.

Vockrodt, Ebba. «Der König D. Pedro I de Castilla in der spanischen Comedia der Blütezeit unter besonderer Berücksichtigung des Verältnisses der dichterischen Darstellung zur Geschichte.» Unpublished doctoral dissertation, Göttingen University, 1948.

Whitehouse, Víctor. «The Theory of the Divine Right of Kings in the Spanish Drama of the Golden Age.» Unpublished doctoral dissertation, Harvard University, 1929.